Passione

Passione

Simple, Seductive Recipes
for Lovers of Italian Food

Gennaro Contaldo

Interlink Books

An imprint of Interlink Publishing Group, Inc.
Northampton, Massachusetts

Contents

introduzione introduction 6

ingredienti essenziali essential ingredients 12

zuppe soup 14

pasta pasta 26

polenta, risotto, gnocchi polenta, risotto, gnocchi 52

pesce fish and shellfish 70

carne meat, game, poultry 94

verdure vegetables 120

tramezzini snacks 152

pane bread 168

dolci desserts 180

indice index 204

ringraziamenti acknowledgments 208

introduzione

introduction

I enjoyed the sort of unrestricted, free-range childhood that few children today can even dream of. The mountains were my backyard. The warm, turquoise sea was a perfect paddling pool just yards away from the house where I was born. The tiny village of Minori on the beautiful Amalfi Coast of southern Italy was my heaven.

School didn't feature much in my life. I played truant constantly, and my days were spent outdoors, fishing with the local fishermen, hunting with my father, gathering herbs from the mountains for my mother, and exploring the countryside. It was the perfect apprenticeship for a chef, and I was already becoming passionate about food.

As soon as I could talk, my large family and our community of neighbors taught me to love and understand the food we ate. Cooking and eating were pleasures entwined in every thread of local life. Good food was central to every family and community occasion.

The excitement I felt as a child, discovering the possibilities of taste and texture and the sheer pleasure of mealtimes, has never faded. My father, Francesco, was the first to inspire me. He was a linen dealer by trade, but was also a great cook. Unusually for an Italian man, he took on the role of main cook in the family. He had a gift for combing flavors and could create an amazing dish from practically nothing. From my father, I learned the importance of using the best and freshest ingredients. He knew which farms had the finest produce and where to catch the best fish, and he taught me to hunt for game.

On Sundays he was in his element. It was a feast day for every family, and he made ours extra special. When the church bell struck midday, all the children knew it was time to run home. I would drop whatever I was doing and hurry through the village to my grandfather's house. What a way to work up an appetite! Glorious cooking smells wafted from every house on the way, and I could detect what each family was going to be eating that day. By the time I reached home, my mouth would be watering.

There were always at least 25 people around my grandfather's big table— aunts, uncles, and cousins, as well as my four sisters, our parents, and me. The dogs and cats waited under the table for us to throw scraps, which flew more generously as the wine flowed freely. The huge kitchen would be filled with the wonderful aroma of smoke from the wood-burning oven. My father was always at the center, holding court and, more often than not, arguing with my grandad about the right combination of ingredients—a matter they both took very seriously.

My father was also serious about wanting me to attend school. It wasn't enough that I shared his passion for food; he wanted me to have an education, too. But I angered him by repeatedly playing truant. There seemed to be so many better things to do than go to school. I liked to go down to the sea armed with a hook and spend the day fishing and swimming. On cooler days, I would set off for the mountains to wander through the forests and talk to the farmers.

My mother, Eufemia, didn't mind my missing school. In fact, she positively encouraged it. She knew she couldn't make me go, so she put my time to good use. She sent me to collect salt from the rocks by the sea, and herbs and mushrooms from the mountains. And she loved it when I went down to the sea and brought home fish. As an ex-dancer, she was a natural performer, and quite a character. Many village people believed she was a white witch. They turned to her for advice with their problems and swore by her herbal remedies. Fortune-telling was another of her talents. She was respected but people were also rather afraid of her powers.

I adored her. Vivacious and exuberant, always great fun to be with, she was a wonderful mother, and I think she understood me very well. She let me have my freedom but all the while she was teaching me about wild herbs and plants as I gathered them for her remedies. We were very close, and I feel proud that people often say I am like her.

When I was eleven, my father decided on a radical solution to my lack of interest in school. One morning, without warning, he dropped me off at his friend's new restaurant to work in the kitchen. I worked from seven in the morning until eleven at night all through the summer. Looking back, it was child slavery. It might have been intended to send me scuttling back to the classroom, but I loved it. Fascinated by every detail, I was prepared to do anything. Although the chef was strict, he taught me a great deal about food. Much to my family's irritation, I began to think I was an authority and started criticizing the way they cooked at home.

Living in a small fishing village, you can't help but be aware of nature and the seasons changing around you. You can watch the weather transform in the distance over the sea. You can smell the changes in the earth and sea with each new season. I love the different seasons. The sense of anticipation as you wait for the cherries to ripen on the trees, for instance. You think you can remember the taste but when you actually eat them after an eight-month wait, the flavor is sensational. Today it feels as if there are no seasons. You can buy any food you want at any time of year. But it all tastes the same. I can't believe it when I go into a supermarket at Christmas and find cherries there. Real cherries are ready in April, May, and June. To me, there is no such thing as a cherry at Christmas.

September has always been my favorite month. The smell of autumn is fantastic. With the first drop of rain, the scent of the dry earth, leaves, and herbs come alive. The wind is fresher and the sea is rougher and colder. In Minori, all the tourists would disappear and the village became mine once again. I would watch the swallows that had been with us all summer forming groups high in the sky, ready to emigrate for the winter. The bats and lizards gradually disappeared and the fishermen brought home a different sort of catch.

Officially, it was time for me to go back to school. My teacher paid personal visits to encourage it, but to no avail. I stopped going down to the sea every day but I started going up to the mountains. The game season was beginning. The fruit was ripe on the trees, wild berries were appearing on the bushes, and there was an abundance of mushrooms. Autumn is the time for finding and preserving food to enjoy in the cold winter months. The mountain farmers were curious to know why I was always wandering around on my own. But they were hospitable and kind. I wanted to watch how they lived, what they cooked and ate, and how they preserved food. I was learning all the time.

The village priests knew all about food, too. They used to eat with all the families in their flock but some households— noticeably the ones with good wine to offer—were visited more frequently than others. They would often move on to enjoy dessert with a different family, this time choosing one renowned for its baking. I was a favorite of Padre Mateo, a very tall priest who looked after the church. He loved children, and used to tell us stories and give us sweets and leftover communion bread. In return, we would do the work around the church for him. He always called on me to carry the cross at the benediction when someone in the village had died. It was a privilege, but I hated the job. I didn't like being in a room with a dead person. It was only made bearable because the grieving families tipped us generously and offered us lots of good food.

I went to England in 1969 at the age of 20. It sounded so beautiful. Every young man I knew wanted to go there. England was cool—it had the Beatles—and I had always been fascinated by damp weather. Perfect. The reality, though, was not the glamorous life I had dreamed of. I found myself working as a kitchen porter at Putney General Hospital. It was the only way I could get a work permit. I was appalled by the terrible meals produced there. The kitchen had beautiful equipment and many varieties of fresh meat and vegetables were delivered. But once the food had been cooked, the result was disgusting. They cooked a dish they called "Italian." I had never heard of it and I certainly couldn't eat it. The pasta was cooked days in advance and then reheated. Vegetables were boiled to within an inch of their lives.

Eventually, the chef grew tired of my constant complaints and told me I could do breakfast—400 boiled eggs and toast. With my poor grasp of English, I set out and, instead of boiling, I poached 400 eggs. No mean feat, I was exhausted, but I think the chef was impressed. After that, I was always allowed to help and, if there was a party on, the hospital would ask me to cook.

By day I was a porter at the hospital, but by night I worked as a chef in Prego, an Italian restaurant in Soho. It was one of the best Italian restaurants of its day. The head chef was Antonio Ruocco, a very talented chef from the same part of Italy as me. I learned a lot from him before moving on to work in two other London restaurants: a private club for City bankers, under a French chef, and Meridiana in Chelsea, where I was trained by Angelo Cavaliere. When I was just 22, I was appointed head chef at the Talbot Inn, a restaurant in the Midlands. From the Midlands, I moved to Scotland, where I trained in English cuisine—and also learned the Scottish way to cook. I loved the Highlands, and went hunting and fishing at every opportunity, until I finally decided to return to London. This time I worked in a fashionable spot in St John's Wood for a couple of years. But at that time, Italian food was still considered a bit of a joke in England. The only Italian foods people knew were spaghetti bolognese and ice cream … and that upset me.

I decided to go back to Italy to learn as much as I could about the food of my childhood. I traveled all over Italy for a year, cooking as I went and learning all the time from the finest Italian chefs—famous ones in the big cities and unknown masters in the villages. It cemented my passion for cooking and reinforced my belief in the value of regional and seasonal foods.

I brought my rekindled passion for Italian food back to England and was employed in many Italian restaurants, culminating in Antonio Carluccio's, where I found myself cooking for the great and good, from royalty to soccer stars.

In 1999, together with my partner Liz, I opened up my own restaurant, Passione, on London's Charlotte Street. We called it "passione" because of my passion for creating beautiful food. It was a small, simple space with a small, uncomplicated menu. I baked fresh bread and focaccia each morning, made my own pasta and preserves, and cooked dishes with wild produce that we picked ourselves. The food was fresh and seasonal and I put my all into achieving perfection. The restaurant went from strength to strength and, after just a few years, won Best Italian Restaurant in London—one of my proudest moments.

Since then, I have been lucky to write cookbooks and appear on TV cooking shows, including my own series, filmed in Italy. All the while, I try to bring out the best of my homeland and, through the wonders of social media, I enjoy sharing my knowledge of Italian food and recipes with the world, bringing a taste of Italy to their homes.

For this, I thank my mother, my father, aunts, sisters, and family friends who helped shape the foundations of my foodie life. At the time, it was normal to talk about food and where it came from and how to cook it—little did I know these mundane topics of conversation would become my life and career.

Whenever I return to Italy, I like to check out the local food. I visit markets for the freshest seasonal produce. I like to visit the family-run trattorie—the ones without a written menu are best! When I go to my home village, I visit my sister, who, at nearly 80, still enjoys cooking for the family on Sunday and when I'm there she cooks all my favorites. I love visiting the fishmonger, the butcher, and the grocery store and can feel my father's presence guiding me to the best choices. When I cook, I can feel my mother's presence so strongly that she might be standing beside me, watching.

I hope this book will bring you some of the joy of my childhood and teenage years. Many of the recipes and techniques I learned all those years ago are still my favorites and you will find them here. Happy reading, happy cooking, and *buon appetito*, Gennaro. xx

ingredienti essenziali
essential ingredients

Anchovies

Preserved in either oil or salt, anchovies are a must in my pantry. I use them in many recipes—a couple of fillets gently "dissolved" in olive oil before adding other ingredients enhances the flavor without giving an unpleasant fishy taste. Salted anchovies need washing under cold running water. The ones in olive oil need no preparation.

Chili peppers

I always keep a few fresh red chilies in the fridge, as well as a bunch of dried chilies hanging up in the kitchen. When I run out of fresh chilies I rely on the dried supply. Dried chilies are more concentrated, which means they taste hotter, so use them with caution.

Dried pasta

I keep at least one type of short dried pasta, such as penne, fusilli, or farfalle, one type of long pasta, such as spaghetti or tagliatelle, and a small pasta shape for soups. This means I can prepare different dishes to suit a particular shape.

Dried porcini mushrooms

You can find dried porcini almost everywhere these days. I generally keep a package in the cupboard to enhance my mushroom dishes, especially out of season, when I crave that "wild forest fungi" taste. Before use, soak the mushrooms in warm water for 30 minutes and then drain.

Vegetables

I like to have onions, celery, a few carrots, and some leeks in store. They form the basis of so many sauces and other dishes that they are known in Italy as *i sapori*—the flavors. They should be finely chopped and sweated gently in a little olive oil at the start of cooking a dish.

Garlic

I couldn't live without my beloved garlic! Look for bulbs with a pinkish-purple tinge to them, as this means they are very fresh. When garlic is fresh, the smell is strong but the flavor less intense. When it is dry, it tastes more pungent. Store garlic in an airtight container at room temperature.

When cooking, I like to crush the cloves roughly but leave them whole, sweat them gently in oil to infuse it, then remove them. I also like to slice the cloves very finely lengthways so they add just a subtle flavor to a dish. Be careful not to burn garlic, or it will taste bitter.

Herbs

Almost all my recipes include some fresh herbs to enhance the flavor. Supermarkets sell all sorts of herbs in packages but I suggest you buy them in pots and keep them on your windowsill, or grow them in your garden. My favorites are flat-leaf parsley, basil, rosemary, thyme, bay leaves, mint, and sage, and I always have at least one pot of each. Besides tasting delicious, they

look great in any kitchen and are easy to grow. Oregano is the only herb I keep dried in my pantry. Instead of chives, I often use the green part of scallions.

Mozzarella cheese

For cooking, mozzarella cheese made from cow's milk (*fior di latte*) is fine, but be sure to buy an Italian make, packed in water. If you find *mozzarella di bufala* (mozzarella made from buffalo milk), then eat it fresh, simply served with a drizzle of good-quality extra virgin olive oil and some salt and black pepper. This is how they eat it in Campania, the home of this wonderful cheese. Or make a traditional *insalata di caprese*: roughly slice the mozzarella and arrange it on a plate with some sliced ripe tomatoes, then drizzle with extra virgin olive oil and sprinkle with salt and fresh basil leaves. Made with good ingredients, this is the king of salads and encapsulates the taste of summer and Italy.

Oils

Apart from Piedmont and Lombardy in the North, everywhere in Italy produces olive oil, so there is a wide variety available. In order for the oil to qualify as extra virgin, the production process has to meet several strict criteria—for example, the olives have to be hand-picked to avoid bruising and then taken to the mill immediately for pressing. Extra virgin olive oil is obtained from the first cold pressing of the olives.

I cannot stress the importance of investing in good-quality extra virgin olive oil. There are so many on the market these days that I suggest you spend a little time investigating which ones you prefer. My favorite is from Liguria. It is not too pungent, but light, delicate, and easily digestible. I use it to dress salads, drizzle over grilled fish, meat, and vegetables, and basically for any dishes in which the oil is to be eaten raw or hardly cooked.

The process for ordinary olive oil is less complicated, and although there are strict controls, they are much fewer than for extra virgin. More abundant quantities are produced, so it is more economical to buy. I use olive oil from Liguria, Tuscany, and Sicily. Olive oil is used for nearly all cooking purposes, as well as for marinades, deep-frying, and preserving food.

Olives

Look for whole, firm olives and always buy unpitted ones. It may take a little time to remove the stones, but they taste much better, since they have been tampered with less. My favorite are Taggiasca olives—small, brownish ones from Liguria. I never buy flavored olives, preferring to flavor them myself with some garlic, chili, and oregano, or pieces of lemon and orange.

Parmesan cheese

This is a cow's milk cheese from Emilia Romagna. I always keep a good hunk of Parmigiano Reggiano (the name for authentic Parmesan cheese) stored in the fridge wrapped in foil or plastic wrap and then grate it as necessary for cooking purposes. Parmesan is also delicious to nibble as a snack when you are feeling hungry, or can be served as part of a cheese selection (see page 203).

Salt

I keep three varieties of salt in my pantry: fine sea salt for seasoning dishes, coarse sea salt for preserving food, and Maldon salt for topping focaccia.

Stock

When I don't have time to make my own stock, I use powder, of which I keep at least one vegetable and one meat variety in store. I find the powdered variety more versatile. It also dissolves much quicker in boiling water. I like the Swiss Marigold brand.

Vinegars

I use white and red wine vinegar as well as cider and balsamic vinegar. I usually make my own red wine vinegar from leftover bottles of wine. I pour all the leftovers into a large glass container, place a couple of pieces of dried pasta in it, which speeds up the process, and leave it opened for about 20 days, shaking it gently each day. After this time, it should turn into vinegar—if not, leave it for longer. I then transfer the vinegar into smaller glass containers or bottles with corks and use it like any other wine vinegar. I find my homemade vinegar much stronger than the bought variety, and delicious on salads.

Balsamic vinegar is produced in Modena, in the Emilia Romagna region. Made from the must of local Trebbiano and Lambrusco grapes, it is cooked at high temperatures until it turns brown and syrupy, then transferred to wooden barrels and left to mature for anything from five to 50 years. This is known as *aceto balsamico tradizionale* and commands very high prices; the older it is, the more expensive it will be. You can buy a cheaper variety of inferior quality, which is matured for only a year and is known as *aceto balsamico di Modena*. This type will do for marinades, when you need a large amount. I suggest investing a little money and going for a five-year-old (or older, if you can afford it) *tradizionale*, to use sparingly in salad dressings, drizzled over boiled meats and poultry, and even over fresh strawberries. You will find that your bottle of balsamic vinegar lasts quite a while, as you need only a few drops at a time.

zuppe

soup

We make very fine soup in Italy. I remember having soup as a child and being able to pinpoint every single ingredient used. It tasted nothing like the bland liquid you find in a can these days.

Every member of my family had a favorite soup. My uncle, the baker, who shared my passion for chestnuts, invented a chestnut soup. It was made from sun-dried chestnuts simmered in water with a single clove of garlic, olive oil, rosemary, and lemon. Amazingly simple, yet so tasty.

My sister, Phelomena, ate soup because she believed it would help her keep her figure. She was fervent in her soup making, and was rewarded with a remarkable balance of flavors that I haven't tasted since. She made the most beautiful vegetable soup.

My mother loved soup because it was a good way of using up leftovers: cheese that was too hard to grate, scraps of meat and vegetables, even pasta. Despite this, her soups always tasted magnificent. My father liked to make game soup, using up all his hunting bounty.

We had soup all year round, including cold tomato soup in the hottest summer months. Over-ripe tomatoes were passed through a gadget to remove their skins, then oil, basil, lemon, and cold vegetable stock were added to the pulp. The taste was phenomenal.

brodo di pollo
chicken broth

Ask your butcher for a boiling chicken, if he has one. If not, use a roasting chicken. The flavor of homemade chicken broth is wonderful, and it is very simple to make: just put everything in a pan and forget about it for an hour and a half. To make it into a soup, either add some pasta for a typical light Italian *brodino* or, for a more substantial soup, add shredded chicken, chopped vegetables, and pasta.

You can use the broth as stock in other soups, risotto, etc. The chicken can be eaten hot or cold as a main course, together with the vegetables, livened up with a little Salsa Verde (see page 74). The chicken is also delicious served cold, drizzled with a little extra virgin olive oil and balsamic vinegar.

serves 6–8
4 lb/1.75 kg chicken
4 carrots, cut in half lengthways and
   then in half again
3 onions, peeled but left whole
6 celery stalks, including lots of leaves,
   squashed and roughly chopped
6 cherry tomatoes, squashed
a bunch of parsley stalks,
   roughly chopped
17 cups/4 liters water
salt

Place all the ingredients in a large saucepan and bring just to a boil. Reduce the heat, cover with a lid, and simmer very gently for 1½ hours.

Remove the chicken and vegetables from the pan and strain the liquid through a fine sieve to give a clear broth. Alternatively, if you prefer, you can leave the little bits of vegetables and herbs floating in the broth. The broth will keep in the fridge for 5 days.

Variation To make an Italian *brodino*, place some of the liquid in a smaller saucepan and bring to a boil, then add small dried pasta or small meat-filled agnolotti (see page 34). Reduce the heat slightly and simmer until the pasta is *al dente*. Serve immediately in individual soup bowls with some freshly grated Parmesan.

zuppa di piselli e menta fresca
pea and fresh mint soup

As soon as spring arrived, we loved to make dishes with the season's new produce, such as fresh peas and herbs. Although the days were hotter, the evenings were still cool, so to keep warm but still have that fresh spring flavor, we would often make a soup such as this one. Try to use fresh peas. It might be hard work to shell such a large quantity but it is well worth it in the end. If necessary you can use frozen peas, or a combination of both.

serves 4–6
2 tbsp extra virgin olive oil
2 shallots, finely sliced
2 oz/50 g pancetta, finely diced
½ celery stalk, finely chopped
8 cups/1 lb 2 oz/500 g shelled fresh peas
1 small iceberg lettuce, roughly chopped
1 large potato, peeled and cut into cubes
4½ cups/1 liter vegetable stock
salt and freshly ground black pepper
15 fresh mint leaves, finely chopped,
    plus a few sprigs of mint to serve
extra virgin olive oil for drizzling
for the crostini (optional):
a pat of butter
8–12 small slices of bread

Heat the olive oil in a saucepan, add the shallots, pancetta, and celery and sweat gently for a few minutes. Add the peas and stir well, then add the lettuce, potato, and stock. Stir well and season with salt and pepper (be careful when adding the salt, since pancetta is salty). Cover with a lid and simmer gently for 15 minutes, or until the peas are tender.

Remove from the heat and leave to cool slightly. Then pour into a blender or food processor and purée until smooth (in batches if necessary). Return the soup to the pan, add the chopped mint, and heat through. Check the seasoning and adjust if necessary.

Meanwhile, make the crostini. Melt the butter in a frying pan, add the bread slices, and fry until golden brown on each side.

Serve the soup drizzled with a little extra virgin olive oil, garnished with a sprig of mint, and accompanied by the crostini.

zuppa di verdure invernali
mixed root vegetable soup

The combination of root vegetables here makes a very tasty soup that is simple and economical to prepare and a soothing winter warmer. Because of its cooler climate, root vegetables are more common in the north of Italy—especially *scorzonera* (or black salsify). This is a strange-looking vegetable, long and thin with a black skin, which needs to be washed well and peeled. The interior is white and has a very pleasant, nutty flavor. If you can't find *scorzonera*, replace it with salsify or extra quantities of any of the other root vegetables used. Parsnip is not an Italian vegetable, but I have included it in this recipe because it is readily available and I love the taste.

serves 6–8
6 tbsp/90 ml olive oil
2 garlic cloves, squashed (optional)
1 small onion, roughly chopped
1 leek, roughly chopped
2 celery stalks, roughly chopped
3 *scorzonera* (or salsify),
   peeled and roughly chopped
1 large parsnip, roughly chopped
1 small celery root, roughly chopped
1 large potato, roughly chopped
1 large carrot, roughly chopped
8½ cups/2 liters vegetable stock
salt and freshly ground black pepper
croûtons and/or chopped fresh chives,
   to serve (optional)

Heat the olive oil in a large saucepan, add the garlic, if using, and sweat for 1 minute. Add the onion, leek, and celery and stir well. Sweat for a few minutes, then add all the root vegetables and cook, stirring well, for a couple of minutes. Pour in the stock and bring to a boil, then reduce the heat, cover, and simmer gently for 30 minutes, until the vegetables are tender.

Remove from the heat, cool slightly, and then pour into a blender or food processor and purée until smooth (do this in batches if necessary). Return the soup to the saucepan and heat through. Check the seasoning and adjust if necessary. Serve immediately, garnished with some croûtons and/or chopped chives, if desired.

> Nearly all of our soups contained a base of legumes, such as chickpeas or beans, since these ingredients could be very cheaply bought from the local grocer's. I remember sacks full of dried beans lined up against the wall of the shop. But these weren't good enough for my mother. She didn't trust their quality because she didn't know where they came from. Instead, we bought fresh beans from local farmers in the summer and dried them in the sun. They were so delicious, I always thought they tasted as if the sun had kissed them. My mother used to store them in jars ready for winter use. I really looked forward to fall and winter, just so I could open the jars and taste the beans again.
>
> Everyone used beans. In the alleyways of my village, you would invariably see people who looked as if they were panning for gold. In fact, they were sifting through dried beans to pick out any stones that had got mixed up with them in the drying process. You always knew they were going to have soup the next day.
>
> When we wanted to use the dried beans, my mother would soak them overnight. The next day, she added fresh vegetables and maybe some dried meat and cooked them slowly in plenty of water. The taste was out of this world. Bean soup is still one of my favorites.

Mamma at our table in the garden

zuppa di borlotti
fresh borlotti bean soup

If you can find fresh borlotti beans (sometimes called cranberry or Roman beans) at the market or your grocer's in spring, buy them; they taste delicious. The pod is the same shape as a fava bean but the color is a pretty cream and mottled reddish purple.

If you can't get fresh borlotti, soak the dried variety in water overnight, then drain them and follow the recipe below. Bear in mind you will need to double the cooking time.

serves 4–6
scant ½ cup/100 ml olive oil
1 onion, finely chopped
1 carrot, finely chopped
1 celery stalk, finely chopped
¼ leek, finely chopped
3 cups/14 oz/400 g shelled fresh borlotti
    beans or ⅔ cup/4½ oz/130 g dried
a handful of parsley stalks,
    finely chopped
3 ripe cherry tomatoes, quartered
1 garlic clove, crushed
6⅓ cups/1.5 liters vegetable stock
a handful of celery leaves
salt and freshly ground black pepper
crostini (see page 155) and extra virgin
    olive oil, to serve (optional)

Heat the olive oil in a large saucepan, add the onion, carrot, celery, and leek and sweat until softened. Stir in the borlotti beans and parsley stalks, then add the tomatoes, garlic, and stock and bring to a boil. Reduce the heat, cover the pan, and simmer for 50 minutes, until the beans are tender.

Stir in the celery leaves, then taste and adjust the seasoning. Serve with crostini and a drizzle of extra virgin olive oil, if desired.

zuppa di lenticchie
lentil soup

When I was growing up, we had a wonderful array of beans and legumes to choose from and lentils were a family favorite. We would often make this soup during autumn and winter—it was a tasty way of keeping warm as well as being a good source of protein. Served with some good bread, it is extremely filling and satisfying.

Lentils were sold from huge sacks and the shopkeeper would scoop out the amount you required. Later, at home, we had to sift through them, since there were many small stones and impurities. I still sift through my lentils today (old habits die hard), although there is no need, as all store-bought legumes are now carefully controlled.

If you keep this soup in the fridge for a day or two it will thicken. Either serve it as a stew or thin it down with a little stock.

serves 4

¼ cup/60 ml extra virgin olive oil, plus a little extra to serve
1 small red onion, finely chopped
1 carrot, finely chopped
1 celery stalk, finely chopped
¼ leek, finely chopped
4 cherry tomatoes, quartered and squashed
1 garlic clove, crushed
1 cup/7 oz/200 g green or brown lentils
1 medium-sized potato, peeled and cut into cubes
4½ cups/1 liter vegetable stock
salt and freshly ground black pepper
a few celery leaves, finely chopped, to serve

Heat the olive oil in a large saucepan and sweat the onion until softened. Then add the carrot, celery, and leek and cook, stirring, for 1 minute. Add the tomatoes and garlic, followed by the lentils and potato. Pour in the stock and bring to a boil. Reduce the heat, cover, and simmer gently for 35 minutes, until the lentils are tender. Taste and adjust the seasoning if necessary. Serve garnished with the celery leaves and a drizzle of extra virgin olive oil.

stracciatella al pomodoro
tomato soup with whisked egg whites

Stracciatella is usually a vegetable or chicken broth with a couple of eggs beaten in just before serving to make it more nourishing. In this recipe I have combined a simple tomato soup with whisked egg whites. Make sure you use good ripe tomatoes. To give it color and body, I have also included some tomato passata. If you prefer not to use the egg whites, you can omit them and you will still have a delicious tomato soup.

serves 4–6
1 lb 5 oz/600 g ripe tomatoes
1 cup/9 oz/250 g tomato passata
   (or puréed tomatoes)
6 tbsp/90 ml extra virgin olive oil
3 cups/750 ml vegetable stock
a handful of fresh basil, plus a few leaves
   to garnish
2 garlic cloves, finely chopped
salt and freshly ground black pepper
4 egg whites
1 tbsp fresh breadcrumbs
3 tbsp freshly grated Parmesan cheese

Skin the tomatoes (see page 139), then cut them into quarters and remove the seeds. Strain the seeds and pulp through a fine sieve over a saucepan to extract as much juice as possible. Add the tomato quarters to the juice in the pan, together with the tomato passata, olive oil, stock, basil, and garlic. Season with pepper and bring to a boil, then reduce the heat and simmer for 10 minutes.

Remove from the heat, allow to cool slightly, and then pour into a blender or food processor. Purée until smooth (in batches if necessary), then return the soup to the pan, check the seasoning, and adjust if necessary. Keep warm.

Whisk the egg whites until stiff, then fold in the breadcrumbs and Parmesan. Fold this mixture into the tomato soup and heat through for about 5 minutes, stirring all the time. Serve immediately, garnished with a few basil leaves.

pasta

Pasta is an essential part of all Italian families' diets and mine was no exception. My mother made fresh eggless pasta at least once a week, usually on a Sunday. The process was a magical and exact performance from beginning to end. First, I would be sent up to the mountains to collect the jars of spring water needed for making the best pasta. I would get into such trouble if I used one of the jars to bring down the newts or frogs I caught up there. Spring water creates the most wonderful, tasty, shiny pasta with the right firm texture.

The area around us was so mountainous that it was useless for growing wheat, so my father would bring back great sacks of the best wheat from his travels around the region. Much to my mother's frustration, he would insist on grinding it himself. The first press was done with a mortar and pestle, then the rough mixture was put between two massive grinding stones, which he turned slowly. When I was good, my father would let me have a turn. It was all very primitive but I loved it; I thought it was real man's work. My mother, on the other hand, hated it. It would drive her crazy. Bits would fly off from the machine and make the most terrible mess, and in any case the resulting flour was too coarse to make good pasta. She went along with it, though, for tradition and to keep my father happy. But when he wasn't looking, she would send me off to the village mill with a sack of wheat to have it ground to the perfect texture—neither too fine nor too coarse. It was a small, incredibly noisy place. They would take your sack of wheat and grind it for you for virtually no charge.

Making pasta was second nature to my mother. She knew instinctively how much water to add, how thick the flour and semolina mixture should be, and how it should be kneaded. She was the keeper of the secret of pasta in my family. She always made the pasta in the evening. It was a relaxing family time and we would gather around the big table and chat while she worked away. She used a rolling pin to roll out the dough and she stuck to three different shapes. The one I most liked watching her make was fusilli. I collected the long, thick canes she needed to shape it (I found these were also good for making kites, although my mother was never too happy when I poached her pasta-making equipment for kite making!). She would roll the dough out into a long sausage shape, then roll this around the stick—it looked such fun to do. She would also make maccheroni and orecchiette using these sticks. On Sundays we had fusilli, but not the short type, a long shape which was handmade. We ate it with a ragu (see page 100), which would take about two hours to cook.

I love dried pasta as well as fresh, and there are some recipes for which only dried pasta will do. It supplies a good, *al dente* texture that is impossible to achieve with fresh pasta. When buying dried pasta, always choose one from a traditional Italian manufacturer.

An unofficial but considerable pasta trade went on between families in my village. Certain individuals became renowned for their pasta-making abilities and their services were always in demand. When my mother was too busy to make her own pasta, rather than go to the shop to buy some, I was sent around the village to barter for it. It has to be said that this was a job I enjoyed. One of the families that made great pasta also had a number of very pretty daughters. Needless to say, I was a very willing errand boy to this house.

My family used to turn up their noses at commercially made pasta but I was strangely drawn to the village's pasta factory. I was fascinated by the massive machines and the dusty bags of flour that were scattered around the floor. The pasta made there seemed to taste better than other commercial pasta. I think it was the combination of fresh sea air, sunshine, spring water, and the care put into making it. The factory was right on the sea front, with big doors that opened out to overlook the beach. I used to hover in the entrance and watch the

teams of men and women at work. Despite the machines, it was still a manual job. The pasta was pushed through the machines by hand and people waited underneath them to catch the pasta as it came out.

After shaping, the pasta was strung across long canes and hung from the ceiling to dry. It was amazing to see so much pasta in one place, all hanging down from the ceiling with people working below. Once it had dried, it was put outside in the sun to harden. It's unbelievable now to think that the pasta was put on an area outside the factory that was really just part of the sidewalk, but people accepted it as part of life then.

Left: Pasta hung out to dry in the streets outside the factory. Below: Making filled pasta with my sister Adriana.

pasta fresca
basic pasta dough

Making fresh pasta is not as difficult as it may seem. I make it twice a day at the restaurant, in the morning for lunch and in the afternoon for dinner. I am well equipped there with electric pasta machines and large work surfaces, so it is obviously much easier to make large quantities twice a day. At home I still enjoy making pasta and I do it the traditional way, by hand, then use a small Imperia pasta machine to roll it out. I recommend you purchase one of these before making your own pasta; it will make life much easier. They are not very expensive and are widely available these days—although when I first went to England, I had to bring my own from Italy. A small pasta machine is compact enough for the tiniest of kitchens and easy to store when not in use. The recipe will work with regular all-purpose flour, but I recommend you seek out Italian "00" flour (also called doppio zero flour); it will yield a better texture.

Makes about 11 oz/300 g
1 cup/5 oz/150 g Italian "00" pasta flour
⅓ cup/2 oz/50 g semolina
2 medium eggs

Mix the flour and semolina together on a clean work surface or in a large bowl. Make a well in the center and break in the eggs. With a fork or with your hands, gradually mix the flour with the eggs, then knead with your hands for about 5 minutes, until you get a smooth dough; it should be pliable but not sticky. Shape the dough into a ball, wrap in plastic wrap, and leave for about 30 minutes or until you are ready to use.

Divide the pasta dough into 4 portions and put each one through your pasta machine, starting at the highest setting. As the pasta gets thinner, turn down the settings until you get to number 1 and the dough is almost wafer thin.

Place the sheet of pasta on a lightly floured work surface and use according to your recipe.

Eggless fresh pasta This is invaluable for vegans or anyone who cannot eat eggs. Simply substitute ½ cup/120 ml warm (not boiling) water for the eggs and make as above.

agnolotti ripieni di carne macinata
agnolotti filled with meat

In Italy this is traditionally made from leftover roast meat mixed with chopped herbs and grated Parmesan. If you want to make meat ravioli but don't have any leftover meat, follow this simple recipe using ground beef and pork. Serve with melted butter and fresh sage leaves, or with a tomato sauce of your choice (see pages 142–143).

serves 4

1 quantity of Basic Pasta Dough
    (see page 30)

for the filling:

3 tbsp olive oil
1 small onion, finely chopped
1 garlic clove, crushed but left whole
4 oz/100 g ground beef
4 oz/100 g ground pork
1 tbsp fresh thyme leaves
a handful of fresh parsley,
    finely chopped
salt and freshly ground black pepper
¼ cup/60 ml white wine
2 tbsp freshly grated Parmesan cheese

To make the filling, heat the olive oil in a small pan, add the onion and garlic, and cook until softened. Add the meat and cook until well browned all over. Then add the thyme and parsley and season with salt and pepper. Raise the heat, pour in the wine, and let it bubble until completely evaporated. Remove from the heat, discard the garlic, and allow the mixture to cool a little. Place in a food processor with the Parmesan and whiz for about 30 seconds, until finely chopped. Transfer to a bowl and check the seasoning.

Divide the pasta dough into quarters and use one portion at a time, keeping the rest wrapped in plastic wrap so it doesn't dry out.

Roll the pasta out in a pasta machine or using a rolling pin on a lightly floured work surface until it is so thin you can almost see through it. Cut it into rounds with a 1¼ in/3 cm cutter and put a small amount of the filling on each one. Fold each circle in half to make a pasty shape and press the edges with your fingertips to seal. Press the filling down a little with your finger, roll it gently over in half, and then fold back the corners (see page 32).

Bring a large saucepan of lightly salted water to a boil, drop in the agnolotti, and cook for about 3 minutes, until *al dente*. Drain and serve with a sauce of your choice.

Alternative meat fillings You could use ground lamb and follow the above recipe, omitting the thyme, or use any leftover roast meat with a flavoring, for example, roast lamb and mint, roast duck and chestnuts, or roast beef with thyme. Simply shred the leftover meat and chop it very finely in a food processor. Add the appropriate flavoring, plus some grated Parmesan cheese. Bind the filling ingredients together with an egg.

conchiglioni ripieni al forno
baked pasta shells filled with cheese

Baked pasta (*pasta al forno*) is very common throughout Italy and includes the popular lasagne and cannelloni. In southern Italy there is a baked pasta dish made for special occasions that is based mainly on rigatoni, with a variety of other ingredients including meatballs and boiled eggs. It is very rich, as most baked pasta dishes tend to be, but I would like to share my lighter version of *pasta al forno*, which is simply based on cheese and tomato sauce. Here I have filled large pasta shells with cheese and fresh basil. You could also fill them with leftover roast meat (see page 34), as an alternative to agnolotti (this way you don't have to make the pasta dough).

If you don't want the hassle of filling shells, you can make baked pasta with any cooked short dried pasta mixed with tomato sauce and topped with cheese. It is also a good way of using up leftover pasta—again, just mix with a little sauce and cheese and bake.

Preheat the oven to 400°F/200°C. Cook the pasta shells in plenty of lightly salted boiling water until *al dente*. Drain well, making sure you empty the shells of water, and leave to cool.

To make the filling, mash the ricotta with a fork, stir in the diced mozzarella, Parmesan, and some salt and pepper to taste and mix well. Shape the mixture into 16 balls, wrap each ball in a basil leaf, and place in a cooled pasta shell.

Pour a layer of the tomato sauce over the bottom of an ovenproof dish and place the filled shells on top. Pour over the remaining tomato sauce, sprinkle over the Parmesan, and top with slices of mozzarella. Cover with aluminum foil and bake for 35 minutes. After this time, remove the foil and bake, uncovered, for a further 5 minutes. Serve immediately.

serves 4
16 conchiglioni rigati (large pasta shells)
1 quantity of Salsa di Pomodoro Leggara
   (see page 142)
3 tbsp freshly grated Parmesan cheese
1 ball of mozzarella cheese, sliced
for the filling:
a generous ½ cup/5 oz/150 g ricotta cheese
1 ball of mozzarella cheese,
   very finely chopped
2 tbsp freshly grated Parmesan cheese
salt and freshly ground black pepper
16 large fresh basil leaves

ravioli ripieni di ricotta e limone con salsa di burro e menta

ravioli filled with ricotta and lemon, served with butter and mint

This recipe comes from Minori, my home village, and was given to me by Antonio, the local pasta maker. Lemon and pasta may seem a strange combination but it is actually very good, and dishes like spaghetti and lemon and black pepper are quite common. When I tried this recipe in England, I found that I had to keep adding more lemon zest and juice. The lemons in Italy are much more pungent, so less is needed. When you make the filling, taste it and, if necessary, add more lemon—the zest only, otherwise it might become mushy.

serves 4
1 quantity of Basic Pasta Dough
    (see page 30)
for the filling:
1 cup/8 oz/225 g ricotta cheese
4 tbsp finely grated lemon zest, plus a
    little extra to garnish
2 tsp lemon juice
2 tbsp freshly grated Parmesan cheese
salt
for the sauce:
1 stick/4 oz/100 g butter
30 fresh mint leaves, plus a few sprigs to
    garnish
4 tsp lemon juice
¼ cup/¾ oz/20 g freshly grated
    Parmesan cheese

To make the filling, place the ricotta in a bowl and crush it with a fork, then mix in the lemon zest and juice, Parmesan, and some salt to taste. With the help of 2 tablespoons, form the mixture into balls about ¾ in/2 cm in diameter and set aside.

Divide the pasta dough into quarters and use one portion at a time, keeping the rest wrapped in plastic wrap so it doesn't dry out. Roll the pasta out in a pasta machine, or using a rolling pin on a lightly floured work surface, into a paper-thin rectangle. Lay the pasta sheet on the work surface with a short edge nearest to you. Put balls of the filling in a line down the pasta sheet about three-quarters of the way in from one side, spacing them about 1 in/2.5 cm apart. Fold the sheet lengthways in half and press with your fingertips between the balls of filling to seal. Cut around the filling with a ravioli wheel or a sharp knife. Gather up all the trimmings, re-roll, and repeat. (It's important to work quite quickly, so the pasta doesn't dry out.) When you have finished, repeat with the remaining pieces of dough.

Bring a large saucepan of lightly salted water to a boil, drop in the ravioli, and cook for about 3 minutes, until *al dente*.

Meanwhile, make the sauce. Put the butter in a large frying pan with the mint leaves. Add the lemon juice and cook on gentle heat until the butter begins to bubble.

Quickly drain the pasta, reserving a couple of tablespoons of the cooking water. Add the pasta to the frying pan, together with the reserved cooking water to help give the sauce a little more moisture. Mix in the Parmesan and serve immediately, garnishing each portion with some grated lemon zest and a sprig of mint.

Alternative potato, cheese, and mint filling This filling is traditionally used in a Sardinian specialty known as *culurzones*. They are quite a complicated shape but the filling is delicious, and perfect for simple ravioli. As a sauce to accompany this pasta, I would choose either Pomodori in Bottiglie (see page 143) or simply melted butter and sage topped with freshly grated Parmesan cheese. Mix 2 large boiled and mashed potatoes with 1 egg, ½ cup/2 oz/50 g each of grated provolone, Pecorino, and Parmesan cheeses, and a handful of finely chopped fresh mint leaves. Use to fill ravioli, following the instructions above.

spaghetti con fave, pomodorini e caprino

spaghetti with fava beans, cherry tomatoes, and goat cheese

This is a light, spring/summer dish that is extremely simple to prepare and looks lovely and colorful. Without meaning to, it has the colors of the Italian flag—green, red, and white. For maximum flavor, do use fresh fava (broad) beans if possible. However, if they are out of season, you can use frozen beans. I use soft Italian caprino cheese, which you can find in good Italian delicatessens. Alternatively, you can use any soft, mild French goat cheese but avoid strong goat cheeses, since they will overpower the delicate flavors of the other ingredients.

serves 4

2½ cups/11 oz/300 g shelled fresh
   fava beans
11 oz/300 g cherry tomatoes, quartered
   and deseeded
7 tbsp/100 ml extra virgin olive oil, plus
   a little extra to serve
2 garlic cloves, finely chopped
20 fresh basil leaves, plus a few
   extra to garnish
½ red chili pepper, finely chopped
   (optional)
salt and freshly ground black pepper
11 oz/300 g spaghetti
4 oz/100 g mild soft goat cheese,
   chopped

Blanch the fava beans in a large saucepan of lightly salted boiling water for 1 minute, drain, rinse in cold water, and drain again. Slip the skins off the fava beans and set aside.

Put the tomatoes, olive oil, garlic, basil, chili pepper (if using), and some salt and pepper in a large bowl and mix well. Then stir in the fava beans and leave to marinate while you cook the pasta.

Bring a large pan of lightly salted water to a boil and cook the spaghetti until *al dente*. Drain and add to the tomato and fava bean mixture, together with the goat cheese. Mix well and serve immediately, sprinkling some freshly ground black pepper, a drizzle of olive oil, and a few basil leaves on top of each portion.

linguine al granchio
linguine with crab

I used to fish for crabs quite a lot as a child but the crabs found on my shore were very small, so to get a meal out of them you had to catch plenty and spend many hours cleaning them.
It was not until I came to England that I discovered the large, meaty crabs on the shores of Cromer in Norfolk. These crabs are excellent quality and what better way to enjoy them than with pasta?

serves 4
2 medium-sized fresh crabs
   (ask your fishmonger to prepare them
   for you and reserve the shells)
12 oz/350 g linguine
for the base sauce:
6 tbsp/90 ml olive oil
1 large onion, finely chopped
1 small leek, finely chopped
2 carrots, finely chopped
2 garlic cloves, squashed and
   finely chopped
a handful of parsley stalks,
   finely chopped
⅔ cup/150 ml white wine
12 cherry tomatoes, squashed
2 cups/500 ml vegetable stock
to finish the sauce:
¼ cup/60 ml olive oil
2 garlic cloves, finely sliced lengthways
1 red chili pepper, finely chopped
the leaves from the parsley stalks (above)
salt and freshly ground black pepper
½ cup/120 ml white wine

To make the base sauce, heat the olive oil in a large saucepan, add the onion, leek, carrots, garlic, and parsley stalks and cook gently until soft. Stir in the crab shells and sauté for a minute. Then add the wine and allow it to evaporate, then add the tomatoes and cook for a further 2 minutes. Pour in any juices from the crab meat and the stock, bring to a boil, and simmer for 10 minutes. Remove from the heat, take out all the crab shells and place them in a bowl. Pour a little hot water over the shells, as if rinsing them, and then add the water only to the sauce. Place the sauce back on the heat, bring to a boil, and simmer for 3 minutes. Strain through a fine sieve into a bowl, pressing down on the vegetables with a wooden spoon to obtain as much liquid from them as possible. Discard the vegetables and crab shells.

Bring a large saucepan of lightly salted water to a boil and cook the linguine until almost *al dente*.

Meanwhile, to finish the sauce, heat the olive oil in a large frying pan, add the garlic and chili pepper, and sweat until softened. Add the parsley leaves and crab meat and season with salt and pepper. Pour in the wine and allow it to evaporate, then add the base sauce and simmer for 2 minutes. Taste and adjust the seasoning. Drain the linguine about a minute before it is done and add to the sauce. Continue to cook for 1 minute in the sauce, then serve.

66 One of the greatest adventures I ever had was while I was trying to catch a tuna fish. I was 15 years old and had gone out with two friends for a day's fishing. We set out to sea in a tiny boat with a box of sardines. It was a lazy, sunny day and we were all just taking it easy when, out of the blue, the thick, brown line we had hanging off the side of the boat started to pull. I took hold of it and realized the enormity of the situation. Whatever was on the other end of the line was huge. The three of us tried to pull it in, but it started dragging the boat down. It was terrifying but exciting. We fought with the fish for about three hours, until it was too exhausted to fight any more.

Together, we tried to pull the 200-pound tuna on to the boat but it was just too big. So we finished it off and dragged it in behind the boat on a hook. I felt sad for this amazing old fish but very proud of myself. I had always wanted to catch a really big fish.

Some fishermen on a motorboat had stopped and made fun of us when we were struggling with the tuna, but I think they were just jealous of our gigantic catch. By the time we got back to shore, word had spread that we had caught an enormous fish and a big crowd had gathered on the beach to witness our return. We were heroes. My mother and father were at the front of the crowd. I jumped on to the beach, my head held high, and my mother stepped forward and gave me a clout round the head, then launched into a public tirade about how stupid I had been. She had been worried sick about me and my father just thought it was funny. Still, it was the biggest fish I'd ever caught and it made me a hero in the village. 99

Old friends Gianni, Rino, Alfredo, and Guido on the beach in Amalfi.

penne con funghi, gamberi e zafferano
penne with mushrooms, shrimp, and saffron

Mushrooms and shrimp may seem an unusual combination but they are quite delicious together and remind me of my hunting days in the autumn. I would pick mushrooms, go fishing, and take it all home, where my father would make a similar pasta dish to this one. The base sauce can be prepared a day or two in advance and kept in the fridge. Don't be alarmed about using the shrimp heads and shells—this is what gives the sauce so much flavor.

serves 4
7 oz/200 g fresh raw jumbo shrimp
12 oz/350 g penne
for the base sauce:
scant ½ cup/100 ml olive oil
1 onion, roughly chopped
1 leek, roughly chopped
2 small carrots, roughly chopped
8 cherry tomatoes, halved and
    slightly squashed
salt and freshly ground black pepper
½ cup/120 ml white wine
½ cup/120 ml water
to finish the sauce:
scant ½ cup/100 ml extra virgin
    olive oil
2 garlic cloves, finely chopped
½ red chili pepper, finely chopped
4 oz/100 g button mushrooms,
    finely sliced
a handful of fresh parsley, roughly
    chopped
½ cup/120 ml white wine
a pinch of saffron

Twist off the heads from the shrimp and peel off the shells. Remove the black line and discard. Roughly chop the heads and shells and set aside. Slice the shrimp lengthways into strips and set aside.

To make the base sauce, heat the olive oil in a large pan, add the onion, leek, carrots, and tomatoes and sweat for a couple of minutes. Add the shrimp heads and shells and season with salt and pepper. Pour in the wine, allow it to evaporate, then add the water. Cover the pan and simmer gently for 4–5 minutes, until the vegetables are tender, then remove from the heat and leave to cool. Put the contents of the pan into a food processor and whiz to a fairly smooth consistency. Strain into a bowl through a fine sieve, pressing the mixture with a spatula to extract as much juice as possible. You should get just over a ½ cup/140 ml of fairly thick sauce.

Bring a large saucepan of lightly salted water to a boil and cook the penne until *al dente*.

Meanwhile, to finish the sauce, heat the extra virgin olive oil in a large pan, add the garlic and chili, and sweat until softened. Add the mushrooms and parsley and stir-fry for a minute. Then add the strips of shrimp, season, and stir-fry for another minute. Add the wine and simmer until it has reduced by half, then add the base sauce and simmer for a couple of minutes. Drain the pasta and add to the sauce, still on the heat. Stir well and cook for about 1 minute. Remove from the heat, stir in the saffron, and serve immediately.

trofie con pesto, fagiolini e patate

trofie with pesto, green beans, and potatoes

I came across this dish when I was in Liguria a few years ago. Trofie pasta is made with durum wheat flour and water (no eggs are used), then shaped by hand into small twists that have pointy ends and are thicker in the middle. This type of pasta takes longer to cook than most; check the instructions on the package, but you will find it usually takes 15–20 minutes. The thicker middle bit always remains *al dente*.

Pesto also comes from Liguria, where delicate olive oil is produced and lovely sweet basil grows in abundance. You can find ready-made pesto everywhere these days but it really is worth making your own. You could use a food processor but when the sauce is made by hand with a mortar and pestle it is slightly crunchier, and you can taste all the ingredients much more. Fresh pesto keeps in the fridge for about a week.

serves 4

12 oz/350 g trofie pasta
4 small baby or fingerling potatoes, scrubbed and cut into quarters
20 green beans, trimmed and cut in half
freshly grated Parmesan cheese, to serve (optional)

for the pesto:

1 cup/2 oz/50 g fresh basil
2 tbsp pine nuts
1 garlic clove
½ tsp coarse sea salt
scant ½ cup/100 ml olive oil (Ligurian, if you can get it)
½ cup/2 oz/50 g freshly grated Parmesan cheese, plus extra for sprinkling
¼ cup/1 oz/30 g freshly grated Pecorino cheese

First make the pesto. Remove and discard the stalks from the basil and set the leaves aside. Place the pine nuts, garlic, and salt in a mortar and grind to a paste with a pestle. Add a few basil leaves and some of the olive oil and grind and stir with the pestle. Continue like this until you have used up all the basil leaves and about half the olive oil—the sauce should become silky in consistency. Then add the remaining oil and the cheeses and mix well together.

Bring a large saucepan of lightly salted water to a boil and add the pasta, potatoes, and green beans. Cook until the pasta is *al dente* and the vegetables are tender. In a large bowl, combine the pesto, drained vegetables, and trofie and a couple of tablespoons of the pasta cooking water. Serve immediately with some grated Parmesan, if desired.

tagliatelle con tonno, limone e rucola

tagliatelle with tuna, lemon, and arugula

This needs hardly any cooking and tastes delicious. When I was growing up in Italy, we didn't have canned tuna but in late spring/early summer my mother would buy fresh tuna from local fishermen and preserve it in oil, so we could have it all year round. Canned tuna in extra virgin olive oil has the best flavor; don't buy it in brine or spring water.

serves 4
12 oz/350 g tagliatelle
¼ cup/60 ml extra virgin olive oil
1 garlic clove, finely chopped
½ red chili pepper, finely chopped
2 x 6 oz/160 g cans of tuna in extra
    virgin olive oil, drained and lightly
    mashed with a fork
a handful of arugula, plus a little
    extra to serve
grated zest and juice of 1 lemon
salt and freshly ground black pepper

Bring a large saucepan of salted water to a boil and cook the pasta until *al dente*.

Meanwhile, heat the olive oil in a large frying pan, add the garlic and chili, and sweat for 1 minute. Drain the pasta, add to the pan along with the tuna and half of the arugula, and toss together well.

Remove from the heat and stir in the lemon zest and juice. Season with salt and pepper, if needed. Serve immediately with the remaining arugula scattered over the top.

tagliolini al tartufo nero
tagliolini with black truffle

A truffle is a fungus, found underneath the ground, which can be detected only by specially trained dogs. There are three types of truffle in Italy: the very expensive white truffle from the Alba region in Piedmont (*Tuber magnatum*), the black winter truffle from Umbria (*Tuber melanosporum*), and the black summer truffle (*Tuber aestivum*), again mainly from Umbria. They are quite ugly to look at and resemble small potatoes, with a hard, black skin. For a special occasion, do splash out on a small fresh truffle and try this recipe.

I dedicate this recipe to my eldest son Michael, who appreciated the subtle but sophisticated taste of this fungus from an early age.

serves 4
14 oz/400 g fresh or dried tagliolini
   (or tagliatelle)
1⅔ cups/400 ml vegetable stock
1½ oz/40 g black truffle, shaved on
   a small mandoline or with a very
   sharp knife
3 tbsp/1½ oz/40 g butter
2 tsp truffle oil
grated Parmesan cheese to serve
   (optional)

Bring a large saucepan of lightly salted water to a boil and cook the pasta until almost *al dente*.

Meanwhile, put the stock in a large frying pan with a few shavings of truffle and bring to a gentle simmer, just to infuse the stock with the truffle. Drain the pasta and add to the stock. Turn up the heat and continue to cook the pasta for 1 minute, until about three-quarters of the stock has evaporated. Stir in the butter and truffle oil and mix in about half the truffle shavings. Remove from the heat and serve immediately, with the remaining truffle shavings on top. Serve with freshly grated Parmesan, if desired.

pennette con fiori di zucchina
pennette with zucchini flowers

I find zucchini flowers a real treat. When I first came to England, I discovered that the flowers were destroyed here so the zucchini would grow bigger. I was distraught! I remember asking an old neighbor if he wouldn't mind giving me the flowers from his zucchini plants. He looked at me suspiciously and I told him they were to decorate the kitchen. I think he would have thought I was crazy if he knew I ate them. Fortunately, you can now find zucchini flowers during the early summer in farmers markets and some good grocery stores, or you can grow your own zucchini! Picking the flowers regularly will help the plants to grow. *Pictured on pages 48–49.*

serves 4 as an appetizer
scant ½ cup/100 ml olive oil
2 garlic cloves, crushed but left whole
2 anchovy fillets
2 small onions, finely chopped
2 small zucchini, finely
    sliced lengthways
scant 1 cup/200 ml vegetable stock
20 zucchini flowers, torn in half
20 fresh basil leaves
salt and freshly ground black pepper
12 oz/350 g pennette (or another type of
    short pasta)
3 tbsp freshly grated Parmesan cheese
extra virgin olive oil for drizzling

Heat the olive oil in a large pan, add the garlic, and cook gently until golden. Remove the garlic from the pan and add the anchovy fillets. Stir with a wooden spoon until the anchovies have almost dissolved into the oil, then add the onions and cook gently until softened. Add the zucchini and stock. Bring to a gentle simmer and cook, stirring, over medium heat for 2 minutes until zucchini have softened, then add the zucchini flowers and basil, and season with salt and pepper to taste.

Meanwhile, cook the pasta in a large saucepan of lightly salted boiling water until *al dente*, then drain. Add the pasta to the sauce, mix well, and stir in the Parmesan. Serve immediately, drizzled with some extra virgin olive oil.

farfalle con piselli, pancetta e ricotta

farfalle with peas, pancetta, and ricotta

This quick and simple pasta dish is very nutritious and a great family favorite. You could use other pasta shapes, such as fusilli, spirali, or penne.

serves 4
12 oz/350 g farfalle
3 tbsp olive oil
2 oz/50 g pancetta, cut into thin strips
1 small onion, finely sliced
¾ cup/4 oz/100 g fresh or frozen* peas
salt and freshly ground black pepper
½ cup/4½ oz/120 g ricotta cheese
freshly grated Parmesan cheese, to serve
  (optional)

Bring a large saucepan of lightly salted water to a boil and cook the pasta until *al dente*.

Meanwhile, make the sauce. Heat the olive oil in a large pan, add the pancetta, and cook until browned. Add the onion and cook for a few minutes, until softened and translucent. Stir in the peas and about ¼ cup/60 ml of the pasta cooking water,* season with black pepper, and cook for 2–3 minutes, until the peas are tender. Remove from the heat, stir in the ricotta, and mix well.

Drain the pasta, reserving 1–2 tablespoons of the cooking water. Add the pasta and reserved cooking water to the sauce. Mix well and allow the moisture to be absorbed slightly. Check the seasoning, then serve immediately with a little Parmesan, if desired.

*Please note, if using frozen peas you may need less water and if using fresh peas, you may need a little more, as well as a little more cooking time.

*Papá, on the right, with his
friends Constatino and Mino
at the local bar.*

polenta, risotto, gnocchi

polenta, risotto, gnocchi

As alternatives to pasta, Italians enjoy polenta, risotto, and gnocchi. Polenta is usually served as a main course or a side dish. Gnocchi and risotto, however, are served as the primo course, which comes between the antipasto and the main course. These three dishes are mainly northern Italian in character and were not very common in our household when I was growing up, although we did have our own versions of risotto and gnocchi.

polenta

Polenta mixed with hot milk was traditionally the staple diet of the poor in the North. This is why we southerners called the people from the North *polentoni* (polenta eaters). When I was young, I thought polenta looked disgusting, and found it hard to believe that northerners ate it daily. I remember my mother occasionally making it for breakfast, but more often than not she used it to feed the chickens and pigs. I now know what a mistake that was, and over time I have come to consider polenta a delicacy. It is delicious accompanied by a heavy meat or mushroom ragu, or simply served with a slice of gorgonzola gently melting over the top.

Cooking traditional polenta well takes a long, long time. Even in restaurants we only cooked it on special occasions, mainly because you have to tend to it for over an hour. The end result is worth it, though. The taste is magnificent after you have added flavor in the form of cheese or vegetables.

polenta concia

basic polenta with cheese

Polenta is coarsely ground yellow cornmeal that is cooked with water until it turns into a soft, creamy mass. Once cooked, it is flavored with lots of butter and cheese and can be served with tomato-based ragu and stews. It can also be left to cool and set, then sliced and grilled to serve as an accompaniment to meat and game dishes. Polenta makes an interesting addition to cakes and cookies instead of ordinary flour, and I use it to sprinkle on baking trays when making bread.

To make the very best polenta, you should use the traditional variety that needs stirring continuously for about 40 minutes. The alternative is quick-cooking polenta (*polenta svelta*), which takes only a few minutes to cook. It doesn't have quite the same taste as traditional polenta but it makes a very acceptable substitute if you don't want to stand over the stove for ages.

This recipe is flavored with butter and cheese. You can omit these for a lighter version.

serves 4
4½ cups/1 liter water
salt
1⅓ cups/7 oz/200 g polenta (coarsley ground yellow cornmeal)
3 tbsp/1½ oz/40 g butter
¾ cup/3 oz/75 g freshly grated Parmesan cheese
¾ cup/4 oz/100 g diced Fontina cheese

Put the water and some salt in a medium saucepan and bring to a boil. Gradually add the polenta, stirring all the time until it has all been amalgamated. Reduce the heat, as polenta does tend to bubble quite a bit. Beware of any lumps forming and, if they do, just beat very energetically until the lumps have dissolved. Stir the polenta with a wooden spoon for 30–40 minutes, until it starts to come away from the side of the pan. If you are using quick-cooking polenta, follow the instructions on the package. Then add the butter, Parmesan, and Fontina, and mix well. Serve immediately, with a tomato ragu (see page 100) if desired.

polenta alla griglia

grilled polenta

Grilled polenta makes a tasty accompaniment to meat and game dishes. It can be made in advance, stored in the fridge for a couple of days, and then grilled when necessary. Topped with some preserved vegetables (see page 138), it makes a wonderful antipasto or snack.

serves 4
1 quantity of Polenta Concia, made without the cheese (see above)
a little olive oil

As soon as the polenta is cooked, pour it into a lightly oiled baking tray. Leave to cool, then cut into slices or use a pastry cutter to cut into rounds.

Heat a charcoal grill or ridged grill pan until very hot, add the polenta, and cook on both sides until crisp.

Alternatively, fry the polenta. Heat a nonstick frying pan until very hot, then brush with olive oil. Add the polenta and fry on both sides until crisp. The pan should be very hot before you add the polenta slices, otherwise they will stick.

gnocchi di polenta con sugo ai peperoni
polenta gnocchi with a red and yellow pepper sauce

This is a different and more interesting way of using polenta by making the mixture into quenelles and serving them in a sauce, like pasta or gnocchi. You could make the sauce and quenelles the day before, store them in the fridge, and just reheat the sauce when ready, adding the quenelles and heating through.

serves 4–6

2 cups/500 ml water

2 tsp salt

2 tbsp/1 oz/25 g butter

¾ cup/4½ oz/120 g quick-cook polenta

3 tbsp diced Fontina cheese

¼ cup/1 oz/25 g freshly grated Parmesan cheese

for the sauce:

3 tbsp extra virgin olive oil

2 anchovy fillets

1 garlic clove, squashed but left whole

1 small red chili pepper, left whole

1 red and 1 yellow pepper, roasted, skinned, and sliced into thin strips (see page 139)

¼ cup/60 ml white wine

¼ cup/60 ml vegetable stock

scattering of fresh basil leaves, to garnish

First make the sauce. Heat the olive oil in a large frying pan, add the anchovy fillets, and cook, stirring, over low heat until they have almost dissolved into the oil. Add the garlic and chili and fry until the garlic becomes golden brown, then remove and discard the garlic and chili. Add the strips of pepper and sauté for a few minutes. Pour in the wine and let it bubble until it evaporates slightly, then add the stock and simmer for 5 minutes. Remove from the heat and set aside.

To make the polenta gnocchi, put the water in a large saucepan with the salt and butter. Bring to a boil, stirring all the time until the butter melts. Reduce the heat and gradually add the polenta, stirring constantly with a wooden spoon. Cook according to the directions on the package until you obtain a medium-thick consistency. Mix in the cheeses and remove from the heat.

Make quenelles with the polenta mixture by taking a tablespoonful of it, scooping it off the spoon with another tablespoon, and then scooping it back again until it is a neat oval shape, turning the spoons against each other. Have a bowl of cold water ready by your side so that the tablespoons can be dipped in the water after each quenelle is made—this makes it easier for the quenelle to slide off the spoon.

Put the pepper sauce back over medium heat. Place the quenelles in the pepper sauce and heat through. Serve immediately, scattered with basil leaves.

risotto

I mastered the art of making good risotto in my years traveling around Italy as a chef. After I left home, I sometimes went back to visit my family and cooked them risotto. They just couldn't understand why you should have to spend half an hour standing by a pot, constantly stirring and adding stock. One of the reasons risotto never really took off in southern Italy was that the climate is so warm that it really isn't comfortable to stand at a hot stove for long.

risotto

basic risotto

The first rule when making risotto is to use the correct Italian rice, such as Arborio, Carnaroli, or Vialone Nano, because they can absorb a huge amount of liquid without breaking up. Next, use good stock and the risotto will taste wonderful. Homemade stock is ideal but a good-quality cube or powder will suffice. Your stock can be any type, depending on the flavors you are adding. For a basic risotto, use vegetable or chicken stock. Cook the risotto at a gentle simmer and stir constantly to make sure it absorbs the liquid evenly and doesn't stick to the pan. Add stock a little at a time, making sure that each batch has been absorbed by the rice before adding more. The stock must be hot, otherwise the risotto will stop cooking when it is added and the dish will be ruined, so keep it simmering in a separate pan. You may find you need a little more or less stock than the amount specified in the recipe, so always have a little extra ready. If you follow these few simple rules then there is no reason why you shouldn't make successful risotto. Just like pasta, it can be a homely, comforting dish using vegetables, or a chic dinner-party affair with wild mushrooms, seafood, or even truffles.

serves 4

6⅓ cups/1.5 liters vegetable or chicken stock
3 tbsp olive oil
1 medium onion, finely chopped
2 cups/13 oz/375 g Arborio or other Italian risotto rice
4 tbsp/2 oz/50 g butter
scant ½ cup/1½ oz/40 g freshly grated Parmesan cheese
salt and freshly ground black pepper

Put the stock in a saucepan and bring to a gentle simmer. Leave over low heat. In a medium-sized heavy-based saucepan, heat the olive oil and sweat the onion until soft. Add the rice and stir until each grain is coated with oil. You will notice the rice becoming shiny. At this stage, add a couple of ladlefuls of the hot stock and cook, stirring all the time, until it has been absorbed. Repeat with more stock. Continue adding the stock in this way until the rice is cooked, which usually takes about 20 minutes. To check if it is done, taste the rice—it should be soft on the outside but *al dente* inside.

Remove from the heat, add the butter and Parmesan, and beat well with a wooden spoon to obtain a creamy consistency. In Italy, this procedure is known as *mantecare*. Taste and add salt and pepper as needed. Leave to rest for 1 minute, then serve.

risotto con piselli, fave e zucchini

risotto with fresh peas, fava beans, and zucchini

All the flavors of spring in one dish! Obviously, if you can't find fresh produce you could use frozen peas and beans. However, do try it with fresh ones, if possible. They are easily available in the spring, and it really does make a difference to the flavor—and the texture, since fresh peas and beans are crunchier. This makes an excellent vegetarian main course.

serves 4

2 zucchini
5 cups/1.2 liters vegetable stock
¼ cup/60 ml olive oil
½ celery stalk, very finely chopped
½ leek, very finely chopped
1¾ cups/12 oz/350 g Arborio or other Italian risotto rice
½ cup/120 ml white wine
¾ cup/4 oz/100 g shelled fresh peas
¾ cup/4 oz/100 g shelled fresh fava beans
4 tbsp/2 oz/50 g butter
scant ½ cup/1½ oz/40 g freshly grated Parmesan cheese
salt and freshly ground black pepper

First of all, prepare the zucchini. Trim off the ends, then cut off the skin in thick strips (a good ¼ in/5 mm thick) and discard the white flesh, which tends to be mushy (you could save it to add to vegetable stocks). Chop the green part of the zucchini very finely and set aside.

Put the stock in a saucepan and bring to a gentle simmer. Leave over low heat.

Heat the olive oil in a medium-sized heavy-based saucepan. Add the celery and leek and sweat until softened. Add the rice and stir until each grain is coated with the oil. You will notice the rice becoming shiny. At this stage, add the wine and keep stirring until it evaporates. Then add the peas, beans, and zucchini and mix well, making sure that the vegetables do not stick to the pan. Add a couple of ladlefuls of the hot stock and cook, stirring all the time, until it has been absorbed. Repeat with more stock. Continue adding the stock in this way until the rice is cooked, which usually takes about 20 minutes. To check if it is done, taste the rice—it should be soft on the outside but *al dente* inside.

Remove from the heat and beat in the butter and Parmesan with a wooden spoon to obtain a creamy consistency. Taste and adjust the seasoning. Leave to rest for 1 minute, then serve.

risotto all'acetosella

risotto with sorrel

Sorrel has a lemony flavor and grows wild but you can also buy a cultivated variety. It's an easy plant to grow in your garden. Usually, sorrel is added to enhance sauces that accompany fish, but its citrus tang also works extremely well with Parmesan cheese.

When we opened my restaurant Passione, I put this dish on the very first menu and it became one of the restaurant's signature dishes.

serves 4

6⅓ cups/1.5 liters good vegetable stock
3 tbsp olive oil
1 small onion, finely chopped
1 celery stalk, finely chopped
2 cups/13 oz/375 g Arborio or other
    Italian risotto rice
5 oz/150 g sorrel
4 tbsp/2 oz/50 g butter
scant ½ cup/1½ oz/40 g freshly grated
    Parmesan cheese
salt and freshly ground black pepper

Put the stock in a saucepan and bring to a gentle simmer. Leave over low heat.

Heat the olive oil in a medium-sized heavy-based saucepan. Add the onion and celery and sweat until soft. Add the rice and stir until each grain is coated with oil. You will notice the rice becoming shiny. At this stage, add a couple of ladlefuls of the hot stock and cook, stirring all the time, until it has been absorbed. Repeat with more stock. Continue adding the stock in this way until the rice is cooked, which usually takes about 20 minutes. To check if it is done, taste the rice—it should be soft on the outside but *al dente* inside.

Remove from the heat, add the sorrel, butter, and Parmesan, and beat well with a wooden spoon to obtain a creamy consistency. Taste and adjust the seasoning. Leave to rest for 1 minute, then serve.

risotto 'terrone'

southern Italian risotto with vegetables

This is the way I remember most people in the south making risotto and how my mother would make it for us.

It does not include butter and Parmesan and you do not follow the usual risotto method. However, it is much easier to make. The end result is similar but without the creaminess you get with the northern risotto. If you like risotto but don't have the patience to stir it for 20 minutes, then try this alternative.

serves 4

1 small onion, sliced
1 small leek, sliced
2 carrots, chopped
1 medium potato, peeled and cut into
   large chunks
2 Jerusalem artichokes (sunchokes),
   peeled and cut into small chunks
1½ cups/11 oz/300 g Arborio or other
   Italian risotto rice
¼ cup/60 ml extra virgin olive oil, plus
   extra for drizzling (optional)
3 cups/750 ml vegetable stock
salt and freshly ground black pepper
freshly grated Pecorino cheese, to serve

Place all the vegetables in a large saucepan with the rice, olive oil, and stock. Cover with a lid and bring to a boil. Then reduce the heat to very low (the contents should not even be simmering) and cook, covered, for 25 minutes. Do check the risotto from time to time to ensure that the rice is not sticking to the pan—if it does, give it a quick stir and add a little more liquid. After 25 minutes, the rice will have absorbed all the liquid and the risotto is ready to serve. Check the seasoning, sprinkle with the Pecorino, and drizzle with some extra virgin olive oil, if desired.

gnocchi

We love gnocchi in the south of Italy. You will find them in restaurants all year round, served plain or with tomato sauce, game, or cheese. I could happily eat them every day.

My father knew how to make remarkably fine, soft gnocchi. You could taste the delicate flavor of the potato through the sauce as the gnocchi melted in your mouth. His secret was his rather dubious source of very tasty potatoes. They were grown by his friend high up on the hill under the cemetery wall in Minori. Every time we ate gnocchi my father would mention this. He said they tasted so good because the potatoes he used were full of fertilizer from the dead bodies in the cemetery. I knew it wasn't true but was still disgusted at the thought. My father would just sit there and chuckle but my mother would get upset and say that he was being blasphemous.

When I came to England, there were many varieties of potato and I was confused as to which one to use. You need a floury variety with a fluffy texture. Yukon Gold or King Edward potatoes work perfectly.

Gnocchi are usually made with mashed potatoes but can also be made with ricotta, pumpkin, or even bread. As they tend to be quite heavy, they are best with simple sauces, such as tomato and basil, butter and sage, or pesto.

gnocchi di patate ripiene di asparagi con salsa al balsamico

potato gnocchi filled with asparagus with a butter and balsamic sauce

If you like potato gnocchi, these are a real treat. I have used asparagus as my filling, because I find it fresh and light, but you could use a variety of ingredients—peas, fava beans, mixed vegetables, meat, mushrooms... As long as the ingredients are very finely chopped, cooked, and mixed with a little grated Parmesan, you have a filling.

The sauce I have chosen is a classic butter and sage one, but I have added a few drops of balsamic vinegar to finish. I find the balsamic cuts the richness of the gnocchi and imparts a characteristic tangy flavor.

serves 4
9 oz/250 g floury potatoes, such as Yukon Gold
1 cup and 2 tbsp/5 oz/150 g all-purpose flour, plus extra for dusting
2½ tbsp cornstarch
2 eggs
salt

for the filling:
1 zucchini
3 tbsp extra virgin olive oil
1 large scallion, finely chopped
4 large asparagus spears, peeled and finely chopped (tough ends discarded)
salt and freshly ground black pepper
¼ cup/60 ml water
3 tbsp freshly grated Parmesan cheese

for the sauce:
4 tbsp/2 oz/50 g butter
a handful of fresh sage leaves
2 tbsp freshly grated Parmesan cheese
a drizzle of balsamic vinegar

Place the unpeeled potatoes in a saucepan of lightly salted water, bring to a boil, and simmer until tender. Keeping the potatoes whole like this means they don't absorb water; if you prefer, you can bake them in the oven.

While the potatoes are cooking, make the filling. Prepare the zucchini (see page 60) and then chop the green part very finely. Heat the olive oil in a small pan, add the scallion, and sweat until softened. Then add the asparagus and zucchini, and sauté over medium heat for 1 minute. Season with salt and pepper, add the water, and simmer for a few minutes, until the vegetables are tender but still a little crunchy. Place the filling mixture in a bowl, leave to cool, and then stir in the Parmesan.

Once the potatoes are cooked, drain and leave to cool. Peel and discard the skin and mash the potatoes (preferably using a potato ricer, or "Italian masher," since this gives a much smoother mash).

Place the mashed potatoes in a large bowl with the flour and cornstarch. Add the eggs and some salt and mix well until you get a smooth but slightly sticky dough. Place on a floured work surface and use a rolling pin to roll out the dough into a thin sheet about ⅛ in/3 mm thick. Cut into rounds with a 2 in/5 cm pastry cutter. Place a teaspoonful of the filling in the center of half of the rounds. Cover with the remaining rounds and press down the edges with your fingers to seal. Re-roll the trimmings to make more gnocchi.

Bring a large saucepan of lightly salted water to a boil and drop in the gnocchi. At first they will sink; as they come up to the surface, cook for a further 2 minutes (remember these are filled gnocchi and much thicker than normal ones, so they need a little longer to cook through).

Meanwhile, make the sauce. In a large saucepan, melt the butter over medium heat, add the sage leaves, and mix in the Parmesan. As the gnocchi are done, drain and place in the butter sauce. Mix together well. Drizzle some balsamic vinegar over the top and serve.

gnocchi di pomodori secchi con salsa alle olive nere

sun-dried tomato gnocchi with black olive sauce

If you like sun-dried tomatoes, you will love this recipe. Very finely chopped sun-dried tomatoes are added to a basic potato gnocchi mixture, worked into a dough, then shaped and cooked in boiling water until they come up to the surface.

serves 4

1 lb 2 oz/500 g floury potatoes, such as Yukon Gold

1 cup and 2 tbsp/5 oz/150 g all-purpose flour

2 egg yolks

salt and freshly ground black pepper

12 whole sun-dried tomatoes preserved in oil, drained and dried on paper towels

for the sauce:

¼ cup/60 ml olive oil

1 small onion, finely chopped

2 garlic cloves, squashed but left whole

scant 1 cup/4½ oz/120 g black olives, pitted and roughly chopped

a few sprigs of fresh thyme

½ cup/120 ml red wine

Place the unpeeled potatoes in a saucepan of lightly salted water, bring to a boil, and simmer until tender. Once the potatoes are cooked, drain and leave to cool. Peel and mash the potatoes, preferably with a potato ricer to give a really smooth mash.

In a large bowl, combine the mashed potatoes with the flour, egg yolks, salt, and pepper. Chop the sun-dried tomatoes very finely, almost to a pulp—if necessary, once chopped, pulse in a blender or food processor. Add the tomatoes to the potato mixture and mix well to form a soft dough. Take large pieces of the dough and roll them into sausage shapes, then slice into ¾ in/2 cm squares. Roll each one over the back of the tines of a fork to mark it slightly and give a traditional gnocchi shape.

Bring a large saucepan of salted water to a boil. Meanwhile, make the sauce. Heat the olive oil in a large frying pan, add the onion and garlic, and cook gently until the onion is softened. Add the olives, thyme, and wine and simmer until the wine has evaporated. Season with salt and pepper.

Drop the gnocchi into the pan of boiling water and simmer until they rise back up to the top. As they float to the surface, lift them out of the water with a slotted spoon, drain well, and add to the olive sauce. Mix well and serve immediately.

gnocchi di zucca gratinati
pumpkin gnocchi baked with butter and sage

This makes a tasty alternative to traditional potato gnocchi, especially in the autumn when pumpkins are plentiful. Pumpkin gnocchi are quite common in northern Italy, and the idea was given to me by Mario, my sous-chef at Passione, whose aunt and mother often make them during the pumpkin season.

serves 6
a pat of butter
1 lb/450 g pumpkin, peeled, seeds removed, and cut into small cubes
1 cup/8 oz/225 g ricotta cheese
1½ cups/6 oz/175 g Italian "00" pasta flour (use all-purpose if you can't find it)
½ cup/2 oz/50 g ground almonds
½ cup/2 oz/50 g freshly grated Parmesan cheese
¼ cup/1 oz/25 g grated provolone cheese (if you can't get provolone, a mature Cheddar makes an excellent substitute)
2 egg yolks, plus extra if needed
a pinch of ground cinnamon
salt and freshly ground black pepper
for the sauce:
1½ sticks/6 oz/175 g butter
12 fresh sage leaves, plus a few extra to garnish
scant ½ cup/1½ oz/40 g freshly grated Parmesan cheese
a few slivered almonds (optional)

Melt the butter in a saucepan over medium heat, add the pumpkin, and stir well. Reduce the heat, cover, and cook until tender, stirring from time to time and adding 2–3 tablespoons of water if necessary to prevent sticking. When soft, remove the pan from the heat and tip the pumpkin into a piece of cheesecloth. Squeeze well with your hands to extract excess liquid. Unwrap the pumpkin and whiz through a food mill, or mash with a fork or potato masher. Leave to cool.

Preheat the oven to 425°F/220°C. Put the cooled pumpkin purée in a large bowl with all the remaining ingredients and mix well to a creamy but firm consistency. If it is too runny, add a little more flour; if it is too stiff, add another egg yolk. Put the mixture in a pastry bag. The opening should be wide enough for the mixture to come out in finger-thick lengths.

Bring a large saucepan of water to a boil. Pipe the pumpkin mixture into 1½ in/ 4 cm long sausage shapes and drop into the boiling water. (Be careful not to burn your fingers with the steam.) When the gnocchi float up to the surface of the water, drain with a slotted spoon and place in a greased ovenproof dish.

To make the sauce, gently heat the butter and sage leaves in a small frying pan until the butter melts. Pour the butter and sage over the gnocchi and sprinkle with the Parmesan, together with the slivered almonds, if using. Place in the oven and bake for 12 minutes or until golden brown. Garnish with extra sage leaves and serve immediately.

ndundari con salsa di pomodoro e basilico

pasta dumplings served with tomato and basil sauce

Here is a dish that comes from my home village and is made each year to celebrate the feast of the patron saint, Santa Trofimena, on July 13. It is said to be an old Roman recipe, and is made in the same way as potato gnocchi but uses ricotta cheese instead of potatoes, making the dumplings much lighter. Each family has its own way of making them but the basic ingredients are always ricotta, flour, and eggs, while the sauce varies depending on what you like. I enjoy these dumplings with a simple tomato sauce (see page 142) but they are equally good with pesto (see page 44).

serves 4

1⅔ cups/7 oz/200 g Italian "00" pasta flour (use all-purpose if you can't find it), plus more for flouring
1 cup/8 oz/225 g ricotta cheese, well drained
3 egg yolks
3 tbsp freshly grated Parmesan cheese
a pinch of ground nutmeg
freshly ground black pepper

for the tomato and basil sauce:

2 x 14 oz/400 g cans of plum tomatoes, drained and chopped in half
12 large fresh basil leaves
salt and freshly ground black pepper
6 tbsp/90 ml olive oil
3 garlic cloves, thickly sliced

In a large bowl, mix the flour, ricotta, egg yolks, Parmesan, nutmeg, and black pepper together to form a soft, moist dough. Place on a floured work surface and knead for 3–5 minutes, until smooth. With your hands, roll the dough into a large sausage shape and then use a knife to cut it at right angles into rectangular shapes about ¾ in/2 cm long.

Bring a large saucepan of salted water to a boil and add the dumplings. Wait until they rise to the surface, then simmer for a further 2 minutes.

Meanwhile, make the sauce. Place the tomatoes and their juice in a bowl with half the basil, add some salt and pepper, and mix well. Heat the olive oil in a large pan and add the garlic. When the garlic begins to change color, remove the pan from the heat and add the tomato mixture. Replace on the heat and cook gently for 4 minutes, until the mixture is bubbling. Stir in the remaining basil leaves.

Lift the dumplings out with a slotted spoon and add to the sauce. Mix thoroughly and serve immediately.

pesce

fish and shellfish

Our house was set on a cliff edge, 100 feet above the sea. I was born there on a stormy night to the sound of crashing waves battering the windows. The sea was the first thing I ever heard and I fell in love with it there and then.

I don't remember learning to swim, it was just something I could always do. I used to swim in the sea every day as a child. I liked to pretend I was all alone on a desert island, running along the shore and screeching like Tarzan, or leaping through the waves like a dolphin and swimming around the bottom of the cliffs with the fish. I would have such arguments with the fish, diving under the water and chasing them around the rocks.

The sea used to come alive with fish in the summer months. Octopus, red and grey mullet, sea bass, bream, groupers, scorpion fish—you name it. I went after them on boats, from the rocks, off the beach. I fished at night and during the day. I was encrusted with sea salt. Even now, if I put my tongue against my arm I can taste the salt.

The sea was part of me and I mastered the art of reading it. It told me what the weather was going to be like, the best time to go fishing, and where to find the finest fish. The secret nooks and crannies of the rocks were my private hunting ground. I improvised with my equipment: fashioning together a hook and line, making my own harpoons, or gathering up cast-off pieces of net from the fishermen. The route to the prime fishing spots was not easy, as the rocks were sharp and dangerous. I learned to scramble across craggy cliff faces and swim through underwater arches to get to my special fishing spots. When I caught some fish, I often built a small fire and cooked them there and then. My favorite was sardines cooked on a stick.

Sometimes I would collect mussels, limpets, and sea urchins. The mussels were small but full of the tastiest meat imaginable, and delicious eaten raw with just a squeeze of lemon. The oysters were even better. To get to the best oysters I had to dive down about twelve or fifteen feet. I learned to take a big breath and pinpoint exactly where they were, then dart through the water like a torpedo and snatch them off the seabed. I ate them straight away, fresh from the sea.

I always took a lemon on my fishing excursions and it served many purposes, apart from flavoring the fish I caught. It quenched my thirst when I was far away from fresh water and acted as a disinfectant if I scraped myself on the rocks. To this day, I always carry a lemon with me. My mother used to tell me that every slice of lemon would give you an extra year of life.

The sea was crystal clear in those coves, and you could see hundreds of small, colorful shrimps darting through the shallow water. These couldn't be caught with a simple hook or net. Instead, I had to make a special trap from very fine net and a ring of metal. It was hard work lying on my front and scooping the tiny shrimps out of the water, but it was worth it because they were extraordinarily sweet to eat and people paid good money for them.

Back from a fishing trip with Gianni (left).

insalata di merluzzo con fagiolini e salsa verde
hake salad with green beans and salsa verde

A wonderfully delicate fish, hake tends to be undervalued in the US, although I believe it has experienced a revival lately. It is eaten a lot in Italy, especially in the South, and in other Mediterranean countries. If you can't find hake, you could replace it with cod. The combination of delicate fish, crunchy vegetables, and tangy salsa verde is really delicious. *Salsa verde* is Italian for "green sauce," and traditionally used to flavor steamed fish or boiled meats and sausages. If you double or triple the quantities, you can store it in the fridge for up to seven days and use it to liven up meals during the week.

serves 4

2 turnips, cut in half and sliced
4 large, flat green beans (such as runner beans or snow peas), sliced on the diagonal into ¾ in/2 cm lengths
4 oz/100 g fine green beans, trimmed
1 fennel bulb, outer layers removed, heart thinly sliced
1 lb 2 oz/500 g whole hake or 14 oz/400 g hake fillet
lemon wedges, to serve (optional)

for the salsa verde:
a bunch of fresh parsley
25 fresh mint leaves
3 anchovy fillets
1 tbsp capers
1 garlic clove, peeled
3 cornichons
6 tbsp/90 ml extra virgin olive oil
1 tbsp lemon juice
1 small tsp English mustard

Cook the turnips, large beans, and fine beans in a large saucepan of boiling water until tender. Lift out with a slotted spoon and set aside to cool. Blanch the fennel in the same water for 1 minute, then lift out and set aside to cool. Cook the hake in the same water as the vegetables. If you are using a whole piece of hake, this will take 10 minutes; if you are using hake fillet, this will take 5 minutes. Drain the fish and leave to cool, then remove and discard all the bones and the skin. Break the fish into large chunks and set aside.

To make the salsa verde, chop the parsley and mint very finely on a chopping board with a mezzaluna, if you have one. On the same board, chop the anchovy fillets, capers, garlic, and cornichons, gradually mixing and chopping all the ingredients together very finely. You could do this in a food processor but I prefer to do it by hand, since you get more texture. Place in a bowl, add the olive oil, lemon juice, and mustard and mix well.

Arrange the fish chunks and vegetables on a large serving dish or individual plates and drizzle the salsa verde over the top. Serve with lemon wedges, if desired.

carpaccio di trota

raw marinated trout

England and the English were romantic visions of my childhood. I used to dream of dressing as an elegant English gentleman—and fishing for trout in my elegant clothes amid the glorious English countryside. I had heard many stories about fly-fishing and, desperate to try it out, I once spent a whole afternoon catching flies and sticking them on to my hook and line. I don't need to tell you that it was a complete failure.

When I moved to England, I was introduced to the secrets of real fly-fishing. I fulfilled my childhood dream and became a master trout fisherman. Winning the prize for the biggest trout in Walthamstow may not sound very romantic but it was one of my proudest moments.

serves 4
2 very fresh trout fillets,
    cleaned and scaled
juice of 2 large lemons or 4 small ones
2 fennel bulbs, very finely sliced
baby salad greens, to serve
for the dressing:
½ cup/120 ml extra virgin olive oil
salt and freshly ground black pepper
¼ cup/60 ml lemon juice

Put the trout fillets in a dish, pour on the lemon juice, and leave to marinate for about 15 minutes.

To make the dressing, place the olive oil, lemon juice, and some salt and pepper in a small bowl and beat well until slightly thickened.

Remove the trout fillets from the lemon marinade and place on a chopping board. With a very sharp knife, cut wafer-thin slivers of trout and arrange evenly on a large plate, discarding the skin. Spoon some of the dressing over and leave for a couple of minutes.

Arrange a few baby salad greens on 4 serving plates, followed by some fennel, and top with the marinated trout. Beat the leftover dressing and drizzle over the top. Serve immediately.

ippoglosso con capperi e dragoncello
halibut with caper and dill sauce

I discovered halibut when I came to England. I loved its light, delicate flavor immediately and it has become one of my favorite fish. I have included two recipes for it in this book: here it is served with a simple green sauce, which gives it a Mediterranean flavor. Serve with boiled new potatoes or fingerlings.

serves 4
4 pieces of halibut fillet, weighing about
    7 oz/200 g each
juice of 2 lemons
salt
¼ cup/60 ml olive oil
for the sauce:
6 tbsp/2 oz/50 g capers
1 garlic clove, peeled
4 anchovy fillets

a handful of fresh parsley
a large bunch of fresh dill
2 tbsp finely grated lemon zest
½ cup/120 ml extra virgin olive oil

Score the halibut skin with a sharp knife, then place the fillets in a bowl and pour over the lemon juice. Leave to marinate for about 15 minutes.

Make the sauce. Place the capers on a chopping board and squash them slightly with the flat of a knife blade. Place the garlic, anchovy fillets, parsley, and dill on the same board and chop all the ingredients very finely, mixing together as you do so. Place in a bowl and mix with the lemon zest and extra virgin olive oil. Set aside.

Remove the halibut from the marinade, pat dry with paper towels, and season with a little salt. Heat the olive oil in a large frying pan and cook the fish skin-side down for 3–4 minutes, covering it with a lid to prevent the oil splashing everywhere. Turn the fish over and cook the other side, covered, for 3 minutes. About a minute before the end of the cooking time, uncover the pan and spread a little of the sauce over the top of the halibut.

Place a spoonful of the remaining sauce on each serving plate, place the fish on top, and serve immediately.

ippoglosso con burro e limone
halibut with lemon and butter

This is an even simpler way of serving really good, fresh halibut. Serve with boiled potatoes and green beans.

serves 4
4 pieces of halibut fillet, weighing about
    7 oz/200 g each
juice of 2 lemons
1 stick/4 oz/100 g butter
salt

Score the halibut skin with a sharp knife, then place the fillets in a bowl and pour over the lemon juice. Leave to marinate for about 15 minutes. Drain, reserving the lemon juice, and pat dry with paper towels.

Melt 6 tbsp/3 oz/75 g of the butter in a large frying pan (keep the heat gentle, as it is easy to burn butter), add the halibut,

and cook for 3–4 minutes on each side. Then increase the heat, pour in the lemon juice from the marinade, and allow to bubble and evaporate slightly. Add the remaining butter; the sauce will thicken. Season with salt, if needed. Serve immediately.

orata in aqua pazza

whole sea bream cooked with cherry tomatoes

This dish is very typical of all southern Italian coastal regions. Freshly caught sea bream, fresh tomatoes, basil, extra virgin olive oil, and garlic—it encompasses the taste of the sea and the flavors of the South. It is an extremely simple dish to prepare and, provided you have the freshest ingredients and good-quality extra virgin olive oil, you can't go wrong. Even if you live in the city and make this dish on a grey miserable day, it will give you the feeling of being by the sea in the warm southern sunshine.

serves 4
¾ cup/175 ml extra virgin olive oil
2 sea bream, weighing about
   1 lb 2 oz/500 g each, cleaned and
   scaled
4 garlic cloves, roughly chopped
20 cherry tomatoes, quartered
a handful of fresh basil leaves,
   plus extra to garnish
1 small red chili pepper, finely chopped
1⅔ cups/400 ml water
salt

Heat the olive oil in a large, heavy-based frying pan over a fairly high heat. Add the bream, followed by the garlic, tomatoes, basil, chili, and some salt. Pour in the water, turn the heat down slightly, and cook the fish for 7 minutes on each side. When you flip the fish over, you will know that it is done if the eye has turned white.

Remove the fish from the pan and place on a large serving dish. Turn up the heat, cook the sauce for 30 seconds to concentrate the flavors slightly, and then pour it over the fish. Serve immediately, garnished with basil leaves, with lots of good bread to mop up the delicious sauce.

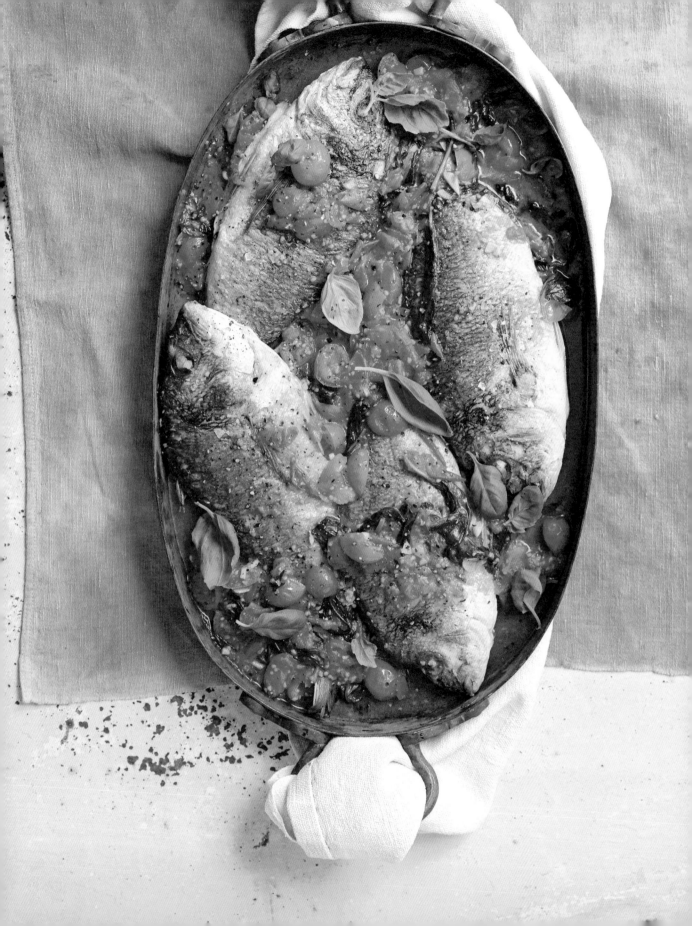

orata all'agrodolce

sea bream fillets in a honey and white wine vinegar sauce

Sea bream is one of my favorite fish and I used to catch lots of them in Italy. The sweet and sour combination of the honey and wine vinegar works extremely well with the chicory and delicate flavor sea bream. Just make sure you have three pans—one for the chicory, one for the sauce, and one for the fish. Try this dish for a dinner party; it's bound to impress your guests!

serves 4
4 sea bream fillets
salt and freshly ground black pepper
6 heads of chicory
½ cup/120 ml olive oil
½ cup/120 ml water
¼ cup/60 ml honey
1¾ sticks/7 oz/200 g butter
1 cup/250 ml white wine vinegar

Score the skin of each sea bream fillet 3 or 4 times with a sharp knife. Season the flesh side with salt and pepper, then set aside.

Cut each chicory head in half lengthways, discard the small, hard central piece, then cut the chicory into cubes. Heat half the olive oil in a frying pan, add the chicory, and sauté over medium heat for 1 minute. Season with salt and pepper, add the water, and cook until the liquid evaporates and the chicory has softened but is still a little crunchy. Set aside and keep warm.

Put the honey, butter, and vinegar in another pan over a gentle heat. When the butter has melted, gently simmer the sauce for about 10 minutes, until it thickens to a syrupy consistency and turns golden brown.

Meanwhile, heat the remaining olive oil in a large frying pan, add the sea bream fillets, skin-side down, and cook for about 3 minutes, pressing down on them with a wooden spatula so the fish doesn't curl up. Flip the fillets over and cook the flesh side for another 3 minutes.

Arrange the chicory on a large serving dish or 4 individual plates and place the fish on top. Pour the sauce over and serve immediately.

involtini di pesce spada con finocchio
rolled swordfish fillet with fennel

The filling in this recipe has quite a strong flavor and I find it goes really well with the meaty texture of swordfish. Blanched fennel and onion give the dish a freshness and crunchiness. It all takes a little time to prepare but it is simple to make and the results are stunning. I would make it for a special dinner. Ask your fishmonger for swordfish loin steaks, which you can either slice yourself or ask him to slice for you.

serves 4

1 lb 2 oz/500 g swordfish steak,
    cut into 8 thin slices
salt and freshly ground black pepper
6 tbsp/90 ml olive oil
2 fennel bulbs, thinly sliced
2 onions, thinly sliced
extra virgin olive oil and
    lemon juice for drizzling
a little grated lemon zest to serve
for the filling:
about ¾ cup/4 oz/100 g fresh
    breadcrumbs
2 tbsp extra virgin olive oil
20 large capers in brine, drained
4 anchovy fillets in olive oil, drained
1 small garlic clove
a handful of fresh parsley leaves
a handful of fresh mint leaves
4 tsp grated lemon zest
freshly ground black pepper

Place all the ingredients for the filling in a food processor and whiz until mushy. Take handfuls of the mixture and make 8 rough sausage shapes with it, then set aside.

Place the swordfish slices in between plastic wrap and gently flatten with a meat mallet or a rolling pin and season with salt and pepper, if desired (bearing in mind that the filling is quite salty). Place a piece of filling on each slice of swordfish; don't worry if the filling comes apart slightly—just keep gently pressing it together with your fingers. Roll the fish up and secure with toothpicks, ensuring the sides are closed.

Heat the olive oil in a large frying pan, add the swordfish rolls, seam-side down, and fry for about 1 minute, until golden brown. Turn over and cook the other side until golden brown.

Meanwhile, blanch the fennel and onions for 30 seconds, drain well, and place on a large serving dish. Arrange the cooked swordfish on top and drizzle with some extra virgin olive oil and a little lemon juice. Scatter over some lemon zest and serve immediately.

branzino con salsa alla rucola
sea bass with arugula

Sea bass is another of my favorite fish and is very popular on the southern shores of my home in Italy—certainly a fish I would often catch. It has a lovely, delicate flavor and deserves a delicate sauce to go with it, such as this one made with arugula. Wild arugula has a much stronger flavor, so I leave it to you whether you prefer to use that or the milder, cultivated variety. If you have some sauce left over, or make extra, add a couple of tablespoons of extra virgin olive oil to it to make arugula pesto and use to flavor pasta as an alternative to the usual basil pesto.

serves 4
4 sea bass fillets
salt and freshly ground black pepper
2 tbsp olive oil
2 tbsp/1 oz/25 g butter
¼ cup/60 ml white wine
for the sauce:
1 tbsp extra virgin olive oil
1 tbsp/½ oz/15 g butter
3 anchovy fillets
2 shallots, finely chopped
1 medium zucchini, finely chopped
1¼ cups/300 ml vegetable stock
10 cups/7 oz/200 g arugula, roughly
    chopped, plus a few handfuls of
    arugula to serve
freshly ground black pepper

First make the sauce. Heat the olive oil and butter in a pan, add the anchovy fillets, and cook, stirring over a gentle heat, until they have almost dissolved into the oil. Add the shallots and zucchini and cook until the shallots begin to soften, then add the stock, bring to a boil, and simmer for 1 minute. Stir in the arugula, season with black pepper, and simmer for 2 minutes. Remove from the heat, allow to cool slightly, then whiz in a blender or food processor until smooth. Return to the pan and stir over a high seat with a wooden spoon until nearly all the liquid has evaporated and the sauce becomes creamy. Remove from the heat and set aside.

Season the sea bass with salt and pepper. Heat the olive oil and butter in a large frying pan, add the sea bass, flesh-side down, and cook over medium heat for about 3 minutes, or until golden brown. Turn over and cook for another 3 minutes. Turn over again and gently peel off the skin. Add the wine, cover with a lid, and cook for a few seconds. Uncover the pan, turn the fillets over, cover again, and cook until the wine evaporates.

Meanwhile, reheat the sauce gently, if necessary. Arrange some arugula on a plate, top with the sea bass fillets, and pour the sauce either over the fish or on the side, as you wish.

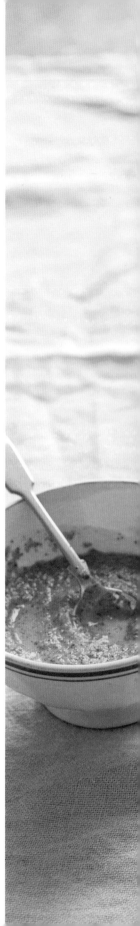

polipo in umido

stewed octopus

I used to love catching octopus when I lived in Italy, and even more so taking it home for my father to cook. It's a shame they are not popular in England, where I live, since the sea is full of them, but it seems they are caught and exported. A great pity, because they really are delicious, either stewed and served warm as in this recipe, or dressed with olive oil and lemon to make a salad. I think a lot of people expect octopus to be chewy and tough, hence its unpopularity. The secret of tender octopus is to cook it without adding any liquid, since it exudes a lot of its own. (There is an Italian saying, "You are like an octopus, go cook in your own juice.") The only liquid allowed is some olive oil to prevent it sticking to the pan. Follow this recipe and you will see how tender octopus can be—it should melt in your mouth.

serves 4

¼ cup/60 ml olive oil

3 garlic cloves, sliced

1 tsp capers

4 green olives, quartered

4 anchovy fillets

1¾ lbs/800 g baby octopuses, cleaned
   (ask your fishmonger to do this)

salt

10 cherry tomatoes, squashed

a handful of fresh parsley, coarse stalks
   removed

Heat the olive oil in a small saucepan (use one in which the octopuses will fit tightly) and add the garlic, capers, olives, and anchovies. Once the garlic begins to sweat, add the octopuses and a pinch of salt. Stir well, lower the heat, then add the tomatoes and parsley. Cover with a tight-fitting lid and cook over low heat for 1 hour and 10 minutes, until the octopuses are very tender. During cooking they will shrink and exude quite a bit of liquid. Adjust the seasoning if necessary, then serve.

cozze 'scappate'
stuffed mussels with tomato sauce

Because I lived by the sea, mussels were part of my life, and as a child I would pick bucketfuls of them during the cooler autumn months. When we had larger mussels, my father would often make this dish by removing the mussels from their shells, mixing them with stale bread, garlic, and parsley and then stuffing the shells with this mixture. Using mussels in this way made an unusual, tasty dish and also meant they would go further to feed a large family. If you like mussels, try this dish for an informal supper with friends; it's fun to eat, as you have to remove the raffia tied around each mussel.

serves 4
12 large mussels
¼ cup/60 ml extra virgin olive oil
4 anchovy fillets
1 garlic clove, thinly sliced lengthways
½ small red chili pepper, finely chopped (optional)
20 capers
3 tbsp white wine
a handful of fresh parsley, finely chopped, plus a few sprigs to garnish
about 2 slices/4 oz/100 g stale bread, cut into small cubes
for the sauce:
2 tbsp extra virgin olive oil
½ small onion, very finely diced
½ tsp dried oregano
2 large green olives, pitted and sliced
14 oz/400 g can chopped tomatoes
salt and freshly ground black pepper

Clean the mussels in plenty of cold water, scrubbing them well and pulling off the beards. Place in a pan, cover, and steam for 2–3 minutes until the shells open. Remove from the heat and discard any mussels that are still closed. Remove the flesh from the shells and any liquid and place in a bowl (if necessary, open up the shells a little more, taking care to keep the shells intact). Keep the empty shells for later.

Heat the olive oil in a pan, add the anchovies, and stir with a wooden spoon until they have almost dissolved into the oil. Add the garlic, chili, if using, and capers. Once the garlic turns golden, stir in the mussels, reserving their liquid for later. Heat the mussels through, then add the wine, and simmer gently for 1 minute. Pour in the liquid from the mussels and stir in the parsley. Remove from the heat, mix in the bread cubes, then leave to cool. When the mixture has cooled, place it on a chopping board and chop quite finely with a sharp knife. Transfer to a bowl and mix well until you get a mushy consistency.

Dry the mussel shells and generously fill one half of each shell with the mussel mixture. Close the shell, removing any excess filling that escapes, and wrap some raffia around the middle of the shell, tying it round a few times until nice and tight, so the shell cannot open (you could use string, but I think raffia looks much nicer). Trim off any excess raffia and put the filled shells to one side.

To make the sauce, heat the olive oil in a large pan, add the onion and, as soon as it begins to fry, add the oregano, olives, and tomatoes. Season with salt and pepper and bring to a gentle simmer. Reduce the heat and simmer for 5 minutes. Add the mussels to the sauce, cover the pan, and cook gently for 20 minutes, turning the mussels over halfway through the cooking time. Stir from time to time and, if necessary, add some water to prevent the sauce becoming too dry. Put the filled mussel shells on individual plates, pour a little sauce over, and garnish with a sprig of parsley. Serve immediately and remember to provide finger bowls for your guests.

Variation: Baked Stuffed Mussels
This is an alternative recipe, in which the mussels are baked and the tomato sauce omitted. Remove the mussels from their shells and prepare the filling as for *Cozze "Scappate"* (see above). Then fill both sides of each empty shell with the mussel mixture. Keep the shells open and place on a baking tray. Mix together a handful of breadcrumbs, a handful of parsley, finely chopped, and enough extra virgin olive oil just to moisten. Sprinkle this mixture over the open mussels. Place in an oven preheated to 400°F/200°C and bake for 15 minutes or until golden brown. Top each mussel with an anchovy fillet and a chopped green olive, drizzle over some extra virgin olive oil, and serve with a few salad greens. This makes an excellent appetizer for a dinner party.

66 As with any love affair, I did have a few rough times with the sea. When I was about 13, I put to sea with a friend for an evening jaunt in my dinghy. We were having so much fun that we didn't notice the wind blowing us further and further from the safety of the shore. We tried to get back but the current was too strong. The people on the beach didn't take much notice of us. When we shouted, they thought we were just a pair of mischievous boys messing around. The truth was, we were stuck.

As it grew dark, we began to get really frightened. The sea was still and the lights of the town were visible for a long time, which kept us calm. But all too soon, they disappeared. I felt the bile of panic rising in my gullet. We imagined we were miles away, and talked about ending up in Africa and never seeing home again. Our young imaginations ran wild, turning the murmuring wind into the whisper of dead sailors, the booming of the ocean into sinister creatures trying to dash our flimsy vessel. We cried like babies as we bobbed around helplessly all night long.

The next morning a police boat found us. When we caught sight of it we started to scream with joy. It was part of a search party out looking for us. We were both severely reprimanded, then they took us home—it only took an hour to get back to shore, so we hadn't gone far at all. I was banned from going on a boat again for a very long time, and my dinghy was destroyed. To keep our dignity, we made up stories of our adventures for our friends—the giant fish we had seen and the dolphins that had saved us. 99

The coastline near Minori, Amalfi Coast.

gamberoni e granchio con aglio e peperoncino
jumbo shrimp and crab with garlic and chili

Always use fresh seafood for this dish. Shrimp and crab make a great combination but if you prefer not to use crab, just substitute extra shrimp. If you find it difficult to extract the crab meat from its shell, ask your fishmonger to do it for you.

serves 4

¾ cup/175 ml extra virgin olive oil

12 fresh raw jumbo shrimp, shell on

4 garlic cloves, sliced lengthways

2 red chili peppers, sliced lengthways into strips

2 large fresh crabs (ask your fishmonger to prepare for you and reserve the shells)

salt

2 handfuls of fresh parsley leaves

1 cup/250 ml white wine

1 lemon, cut into quarters, to serve

slices of bread, to serve

Heat the olive oil in a large frying pan, add the shrimp, and cook for 1 minute over high heat. Turn them over and cook the other side for another minute. Add the garlic, chilies, and crab chunks, season with salt, then reduce the heat and cook for 2 minutes with the lid on. Add the parsley, increase the heat, and pour in the wine and any reserved juices from the crab. Bubble until evaporated, then serve immediately, with lemon quarters and lots of bread to mop up the juices.

Minori was a fishing village. I used to hang around the fishermen when they came back with their catches, learning from them, teasing them, and probably driving them crazy.

Every afternoon my friends and I waited on the beach for the fishermen to return from their trips. Quite often they would bring ashore a mighty turtle, which they had untangled from their nets. The poor creature would be half dead and brought back as a novelty. They may have caught it a few days earlier but they would have tied it to the back of the boat and dragged it to shore as a trophy. Sometimes the well-traveled sailors would take the turtles home to eat, and many people used their shells to decorate their houses. I never liked this. I knew instinctively that these beasts needed protecting.

One day I was alone on the beach when one of the fishing boats returned with a turtle in a poor state, but still alive. I asked the fishermen if I could have it and, using all my strength, I dragged the half-dead beast back into the sea and round to a small cove away from the main beach. I stayed with her all afternoon, willing her to recover her strength. At night I found a rope and tied her to a rock in the cover. The next morning, when I rushed down to check on her, I found to my joy that she was full of life and spirit, flapping around to try and free herself. I cut the rope and watched her swim away effortlessly.

After that, the turtles became my mission. Every time a fisherman brought one ashore, I would try to save it, though usually without as much success. To my relief, the fishermen soon began to understand that the turtles were special and stopped bringing them home.

pesce conservato
preserved fish

Preserving fish is an old tradition and, although its original purpose was to deal with a large catch, preserved fish is still eaten today as a delicacy rather than out of necessity. Here are some of the most popular preserved fish used in Italian cooking.

Acciughe
You can buy anchovies preserved in either oil or salt. For both types, fresh anchovies are gutted, layered with sea salt, and left for about a month. They are then filleted and packed in jars or rinsed of the salt and placed in jars or cans with olive or vegetable oil. See page 12 for tips on using anchovies in cooking.

Baccalá
This is cod preserved in salt. It was traditionally known as "poor food," and was eaten by people who lived inland and did not have access to the sea. Cod was the cheapest fish available and was preserved in large quantities, then kept in the pantry. However, it has become quite fashionable these days and commands a high price.

You can buy *baccalá* in pieces, which need to be soaked in several changes of fresh water for at least 24 hours before use, thereby removing the salt and softening the flesh. In some areas of Italy, such as Liguria, Venice, and Naples, baccalá is very prominent on the menu. It is delicious steamed or boiled, then simply dressed with some extra virgin olive oil and lemon juice, eaten warm or cold as a salad, or cooked in a tomato sauce with black olives. It also makes delicious fish cakes and fritters.

Bottarga
This is cured roe of grey mullet and tuna, produced and consumed mainly in Sicily and Sardinia. It can be used like *mosciame* (see below), but is more commonly grated over seafood pasta dishes. You can find it in good Italian delicatessens.

Mosciame
This air-dried fillet of tuna has become quite a delicacy on many menus. It is available in Italian or Spanish delicatessens. Serve thinly sliced, drizzled with some extra virgin olive oil and lemon juice, and accompanied by preserved vegetables (see page 138) as an alternate antipasto to cured meats.

Pesce affumicato
Smoked fish is becoming increasingly popular in Italy and swordfish, tuna, halibut, and sturgeon are just some of the varieties available. Arrange an assortment of thinly sliced smoked fish on a large plate, drizzle with lemon juice, and serve with mixed baby salad greens and arugula for an antipasto or light lunch.

Stoccafisso
This is air-dried cod. It is sold whole and should be soaked in several changes of fresh water for about 24 hours before use. It also helps to tenderize it if you bash it with a mallet before soaking. Cook it in the same way as *baccalá* (see above).

carne

meat, game, poultry

The backyard of my childhood home was like a small farmyard. There were chickens scratching about in the dirt, lots of rabbits, and guinea pigs, and we always had a pig. Every Sunday, we bought meat from one of the three village butchers. We only ate meat once or twice a week but it was truly fresh and we knew where it came from, whether it was the farm or our own backyard. Markets full of live animals—rabbits, chickens, lambs, and cows—were part of our lives. We saw animals as a source of food, yet we cared for them and loved them as if they were our pets.

Every Thursday, a bullock was slaughtered in Minori. It was a fascinating event for the children. Great groups of us used to sit on the slaughterhouse wall to watch the gruesome spectacle. The butcher was a bull of a man himself, with a jutting chin. The killing was so cruel and brutal that to our childish eyes it looked like the crucifixion of Jesus. The butcher would tie the bullock's head to a post and bash it hard with a large mallet. Then he slit its throat and drained off all the blood. Finally the bullock was lifted up with large, heavy chains to be gutted and skinned.

People are so removed from the source of their meat these days. You go into a supermarket and see endless rows of pre-packaged poultry, meat, and game. It's difficult to associate meat with live animals. For me, it was part of my culture. We respected animals because we knew they were our food. I never saw my mother buy a chicken or pigeon at the butcher's. She had a pigeon coop and she would take the birds out as she needed them.

By the time I was 11, my father was wise enough to see where my heart lay. During the summer holidays, he found me a job in a fine restaurant run by one of his friends—a great chef by the name of Alfonso. I adored the job, but I think I must have been rather a handful, if only because of my boundless enthusiasm.

As a very junior waiter, I was permitted to greet customers and tell them what was on the menu, but I was not yet entrusted with the important task of taking orders. However, I invented a special responsibility of my own. Almost immediately, I discovered that I could predict people's orders from their reaction when I recited the menu. I would run straight into the kitchen and prepare the ingredients necessary for those dishes, ready for the chef to cook them. Alfonso thought he was losing his mind when, time after time, he went to the preparation table only to find his work already done. He was afraid he had done it himself and then forgotten about it. Eventually he caught me in the act and, after much shouting and swearing, he banned me from the kitchen for the rest of the day. Later, he calmed down, and when he realized how keen I was to cook, he found me work in the kitchen.

Alfonso's restaurant had chickens, rabbits, and sometimes even lambs in the backyard. We killed what we needed each day. If the chef ran out of chicken in the middle of a shift, I'd have to run out and prepare another. It might sound gruesome but it meant that all our meat was very fresh.

My time in the kitchen taught me about every sort of meat and every way to cook it. I learned not to waste anything; we used every last scrap.

Me, at 8 years old.

antipasto di pesche e prosciutto crudo di parma

antipasto of fresh peaches and prosciutto

Prosciutto with melon, prosciutto with figs … both wonderful combinations, but in the middle of a warm summer why not with peaches? It makes a lovely and refreshing appetizer, but you must use ripe peaches. If you can find them, the small organic ones are out of this world. I dedicate this recipe to Dominique, who loves prosciutto so much she would have it at every meal.

serves 1
1 ripe peach
a few slices of prosciutto di Parma,
    very thinly and freshly cut
a handful of arugula
extra virgin olive oil
freshly ground black pepper

Remove the skin from the peach—this is made easier by immersing the peach in boiling water for a minute. Cut the peach in half and discard the pit. Arrange on a plate with the prosciutto and arugula. Drizzle with some extra virgin olive oil and grind over some black pepper.

polpette al vapore

steamed meatballs

This dish has great sentimental value for me, since my mother would cook it when I was recovering from an illness. Because the meatballs are steamed and not fried, they are gentle on the stomach and easy to digest. It's also a good way to enjoy meatballs without the added fat! Use the best lean ground beef you can find—ground steak is ideal.

serves 4–6
2 tbsp extra virgin olive oil
3 tbsp water
1 lb 2 oz/500 g very lean ground beef
2 garlic cloves, very finely chopped
a handful of fresh parsley,
    very finely chopped
salt and freshly ground black pepper

Half fill a pan with water and bring to a boil. Cover with a plate roughly the same size as the pan, or just a little larger, and put half the olive oil and the 3 tablespoons of water on the plate.

Meanwhile, in a large bowl, mix together the meat, garlic, parsley, the remaining olive oil, and some salt and pepper. It is much easier to do this with your hands. When all the ingredients are well combined, shape into about 25 small balls.

When the water begins to boil, turn down the heat to medium, so the water is gently simmering. Place the meatballs on the plate on top of the pan and cover with an upturned plate or, ideally, a glass bowl so that you can see through it.

Leave to steam for 30 minutes, turning the meatballs over halfway through. Serve immediately, as the meat tends to toughen slightly when cool. You can serve the meatballs with pasta or on their own, with some good bread to mop up the liquid.

vitello alla genovese
slow-cooked veal with onions

This is an old recipe from the Campania region, and not from Genoa as the name suggests. In the days of the old Italian maritime republics (Genoa, Amalfi, Venice, and Pisa), this dish was made for Genoese sailors when they docked in Amalfi, hence the name. Although it takes three hours to cook, it is an extremely straightforward dish to make and you get two courses from just one pot. The onion sauce is used to flavor pasta as an appetizer, or primo, and the veal is served as a main course. Try it for a different roast lunch.

serves 4–6
2¼ lb/1 kg veal bottom round roast
salt and freshly ground black pepper
3 garlic cloves, sliced
a handful of fresh parsley, roughly torn
⅔ cup/150 ml olive oil
5½ lb/2.5 kg large onions, sliced
1 celery stalk, diced
1 carrot, diced
1 bunch of rosemary sprigs, 2 bay leaves, and 2 sage leaves, tied together to make a bouquet garni
scant 1 cup/200 ml white wine
to serve:
cooked pennette or other tubular pasta
freshly grated Parmesan cheese
green salad

Place the veal joint on a chopping board. With a sharp knife, unroll it until you obtain a long, flat piece, then put skin-side down. Season with salt and pepper, rubbing them well into the meat, followed by the garlic and parsley. Roll up again and tie together with 4 pieces of string, trimming off any excess.

Heat the olive oil in a large saucepan, add the veal, and sear on all sides. Remove from the pan and set aside. Add the onions, celery, and carrot to the pan, season with salt and pepper, and stir well. Add the bouquet garni and cook until the onions begin to soften. Put the veal back in the pan, cover with a lid, then reduce the heat to low and cook for 3 hours, until very tender. Stir the onions and turn the meat from time to time to prevent sticking. After 3 hours, turn up the heat, add the wine, and simmer for 5 minutes. Remove the meat from the pan and set aside. With a potato masher, mash the onions slightly. Taste and adjust the seasoning.

Serve the onion sauce with the cooked pasta and some freshly grated Parmesan. For the main course, slice the veal and serve with a little of the sauce and a green salad.

il ragu
stuffed beef rolls in tomato ragu

This recipe takes me back to my childhood Sunday lunches and, more recently, to family gatherings when I return to my home village. My Aunt Maria was the "queen" of this dish and would spend the entire morning checking, stirring, and making sure it was just right for all the family to enjoy. It is traditionally made every Sunday in all regions of southern Italy. It is a simple dish to prepare and takes about two hours to cook—some traditionalists will cook it for longer to get an even richer tomato sauce, but if you follow this recipe two hours will suffice. The tomato sauce is used to flavor pasta for the *primo* (pasta course) and the meat is eaten as a *secondo* (main course). Any leftover sauce can be used to flavor pasta dishes throughout the week.

serves 6
12 small thin sirloin steaks
salt and freshly ground black pepper
¼ cup/1 oz/25 g freshly grated Parmesan
    cheese
4 garlic cloves, finely chopped
a handful of fresh parsley, torn
for the sauce:
6 tbsp/90 ml olive oil
⅔ cup/150 ml red wine
1 onion, very finely chopped
1 celery stalk, very finely chopped
2 tbsp tomato paste, diluted in
    1⅔ cups/400 ml lukewarm water
2 x 14 oz/400 g cans of chopped
    tomatoes
a handful of fresh basil leaves
cooked tagliatelle or rigatoni to serve

Arrange the slices of meat on a chopping board or a clean work surface and flatten them with a meat tenderizer (if you don't have one, place a flat wooden spatula over the meat and bash with the palm of your hand). Season with salt and pepper, then sprinkle with the grated Parmesan, garlic, and parsley. Roll each slice up tightly and secure well with toothpicks.

For the sauce, heat the olive oil in a large saucepan. When hot, lower the heat, add the meat rolls, and sear well on all sides. Increase the heat again, add the wine, and simmer until it has reduced by half. Remove the meat and set aside.

Add the onion and celery to the pan and stir well. Cook until the remainder of the wine has nearly evaporated, then put the meat back in the pan and pour over the diluted tomato paste and the chopped tomatoes. Season with salt and pepper and stir in the basil. Lower the heat and partially cover with a lid. Cook gently for 2 hours, stirring from time to time. Check the seasoning.

Serve the tomato sauce with cooked pasta. Then serve the meat rolls as a main course with a green salad.

cotolette di agnello alla griglia ripiene di prosciutto ed erbe

grilled lamb chops filled with prosciutto and herbs

You can make the filling in advance, or make lots of it and store some in the fridge or freezer for another time. When choosing lamb chops, go to a reliable butcher and ask for organic (if available) or the best-quality racks of lamb. Usually one rack of lamb contains approximately six chops.

serves 4
10 fresh sage leaves
a handful of fresh rosemary needles
a handful of fresh parsley leaves
a handful of fresh basil leaves
1 garlic clove, finely chopped
⅓ cup/1 oz/30 g freshly grated Parmesan cheese
1 stick/4 oz/100 g butter, slightly softened (remove from the fridge about an hour before using)
salt and freshly ground black pepper
6 slices of prosciutto di Parma
12 lamb rib chops

Place all the herbs on a chopping board and chop very finely together. Place them in a bowl with the garlic, Parmesan, butter, and some salt and pepper and mix well until you get a smooth paste.

Arrange the prosciutto slices overlapping slightly on a piece of plastic wrap and spread the paste evenly over them with a spatula. Then, with the help of the plastic wrap, roll up the ham into a sausage shape, encased in the plastic wrap, and tie the ends so the filling doesn't escape. Place in the fridge for at least an hour.

Slice each lamb chop horizontally through the center, leaving it joined at one end, and open it up like a butterfly. With a meat tenderizer, flatten each piece. (You can ask your butcher to do this for you if you prefer.)

Remove the filling from the fridge and discard the plastic wrap. Cut the filling into 1 in/2.5 cm slices, pressing slightly to flatten. Place on one side of each cutlet and fold the other side over the top. Press together well, making sure that none of the filling escapes. Transfer the cutlets to a baking tray lined with foil and season with salt and pepper.

Place under a hot broiler and cook for about 2 minutes on each side for rare, 4 minutes for medium or, for well done, as long as you like! Serve immediately with Patate Saltate (see page 124).

I have always loved animals. My father kept cats and dogs and I grew up surrounded by a whole range of farmyard creatures, which became my playmates. But I soon learned not to become too attached to them.

Every Easter, my father would return from his travels laden with goodies for our traditional spring feast: the finest goat, chicken, capon, and lamb, raised by his farmer friends. To make sure he was getting the freshest meat and the finest quality, he would make a point of seeing each animal alive before he bought it.

One year he made his mistake. A couple of weeks before Easter, he accepted a baby goat as payment for an old debt. It was just a few weeks old but he knew it would be perfect for our Easter lunch. He also thought it would be fun for me to have a baby goat to play with. To be fair to my father, he did tell me that it was our Easter lunch, but I was just a small child and really didn't want to believe such a brutal truth, so I pushed it to the back of my mind.

Looking after this hungry kid was a 24-hour-a-day job. I called him Bottiglia (Bottle) because I fed him milk from a bottle. He quickly became my whole life. My family and friends teased me mercilessly but I loved him. Bottiglia was my friend, constant companion, and confidant. I created a wonderful adventure dream world in my head for the two of us. He came with me to the beach, trotted behind me on my jaunts to the mountains, and wandered through the village streets with me. He was my little shadow, and I believe he loved me as much as I loved him. I was his surrogate mother and he was my pride and joy.

It came to school time and I kicked up a fuss. I didn't want to leave my new best friend at home but my parents threatened me, saying that if I didn't go to school they would take him away. For two weeks I went to school every day without fail and without complaint. I didn't want to lose Bottiglia.

The day before Easter, I ran home from school and straight through the house to find him. I had been thinking all day about Bottiglia and the adventures we could have. I was so looking forward to seeing him … and there he was, hanging by his back legs from the ceiling, his throat cut and blood still dripping from his neck. I couldn't believe the horror in front of my eyes. Even now, it still counts as the worst day of my life. I started to cry, and my mother shouted at my father, telling him he shouldn't have done it, knowing how much I loved the goat. My father would have none of it. As far as he was concerned, he had done nothing wrong. He walloped me for crying and said I was old enough to know better than to get attached to food.

The next day at lunch I felt sick. I couldn't eat my friend but I had to sit and watch everyone else tucking in. I'll never forget my little sister laughing at me, and the rest of the table joining in.

Although this might seem harsh, ultimately my father was right. The kid was always intended as our Easter meal. It was a valuable lesson. From that moment, I still loved animals but I also respected them as a source of food. 99

porchetta

stuffed rolled pork belly

Traditionally in Italy, *porchetta* is a whole piglet filled with lots of fresh herbs and slow-roasted either in a wood oven or outdoors on a spit. It is made at home or sold ready-made as takeout, and you can buy it whole, a few slices, or just have a slice between bread as a sandwich. As whole piglets are not that easily obtainable, I use pork belly and the result is the same. It is simple to prepare and can be made in advance and eaten cold—a good idea for parties or to feed a large group of people for Sunday lunch.

serves 10–12

11 lb/5 kg piece of pork belly—ask the butcher to remove the ribs and trim off the excess fat
1½ tbsp coarse salt
coarsely ground black pepper
leaves from a large bunch of fresh thyme
needles from a large bunch of fresh rosemary, roughly chopped
a large bunch of fresh sage leaves, roughly chopped
1 tbsp fennel seeds (if you are lucky enough to find wild fennel, use it instead, finely chopped—its flavor is unique)
8 garlic cloves, finely chopped
2 tbsp olive oil
6 tbsp/90 ml clear honey

Preheat the oven to its highest setting. Lay the pork belly skin-side down. Sprinkle half the salt and lots of coarsely ground black pepper over it, rubbing them well into the meat with your fingers. Leave to rest for 10 minutes so the salt and pepper settle well into the meat. Then sprinkle the herbs, fennel seeds, and garlic evenly all over it.

Next tie up the meat. You will need 10 pieces of string, each about 12 in/ 30 cm long. Carefully roll the meat up widthways and tie it very tightly with string in the middle of the joint. Then tie at either end about ½ in/1 cm from the edge, and keep tying along the joint until you have used up all the string. The filling should be well wrapped—if any excess filling escapes from the sides, push it in. With your hands, massage 1 tablespoon of the olive oil all over the meat. Then rub the remaining salt over it with some more black pepper.

Grease a large roasting pan with the remaining olive oil and place the pork in it. Roast for 10 minutes, then turn it over. After 15 minutes, reduce the oven temperature to 300°F/150°C and cover the meat with aluminum foil. (If you like the rind very crisp, don't bother with the foil, but remember that the *porchetta* needs to be sliced thinly and crispy skin will make this difficult.) Roast for 3 hours.

Remove the meat from the oven and coat with the honey, drizzling some of the juices from the roasting pan all over it, too. Insert a fork in either side of the meat and lift it onto a wooden board. If you are serving the *porchetta* immediately, place the roasting pan on the stovetop and stir with a wooden spoon, scraping up all the caramelized bits from the base of the pan, until the juices from the meat reduce and thicken slightly. Slice the meat thinly and serve with the sauce. Alternatively, leave the meat to cool and slice when needed. It will keep for up to a week in the fridge.

polletto in agrodolce

baby chicken in a cider vinegar sauce

Baby chickens (poussins) are much more tender than a fully matured one. They also look more attractive when served. You can choose whether to serve a whole one or half per person, depending on people's appetite and the size (look for small ones for this recipe). If you are serving an appetizer and accompaniments, then one poussin between two people is sufficient.

serves 2–4

2 small baby chickens (poussins), deboned (ask your butcher to do this for you)
salt and freshly ground black pepper
6 tbsp/90 ml olive oil
scattering of fresh parsley,
    to serve (optional)

for the filling:

2 garlic cloves, peeled
2 tbsp capers
1 tsp sea salt
2 tsp extra virgin olive oil
needles from 2 sprigs of fresh rosemary
a handful of chopped fresh parsley
freshly ground black pepper

for the sauce:

2 garlic cloves, peeled
needles from 2 sprigs of fresh rosemary
½ cup/120 ml white wine
½ cup/120 ml cider vinegar
½ tbsp sugar
1 tbsp capers

First make the filling by placing all the ingredients in a mortar and pounding them with a pestle until you obtain a pulp.

Open up each baby chicken like a butterfly and place skin-side down on a chopping board. Spread the filling evenly over the flesh side, then fold the chicken back over and secure the opening with wooden toothpicks, weaving them in and out. Season all over with salt and pepper. Heat the olive oil in a large frying pan, add the chickens, then reduce the heat slightly and cook until golden brown on all sides. Cover the pan and cook gently for about 20 minutes, until the chickens are cooked through.

Meanwhile, make the sauce. Place the garlic and rosemary in a mortar and pound with a pestle. Add the wine, vinegar, sugar, and capers, and mix well.

Turn up the heat under the chickens, add the sauce, and simmer until reduced by half, stirring all the time. Arrange on a plate and pour over the sauce. Serve immediately, scattered with parsley, if desired.

petti di pollo con limone e timo

chicken breasts with lemon and thyme

Oh, the taste of my childhood: chickens scratching in the backyard, lemons and thyme from the garden. A distant but very vivid memory. Try this recipe with free-range or corn-fed chicken breasts—the combination with lemon and fresh thyme is wonderful. Serve with boiled potatoes and green beans.

serves 4
⅔ cup/150 ml white wine
juice of 1 lemon
4 boneless chicken breasts
salt and freshly ground black pepper
all-purpose flour, for dusting
½ cup/120 ml olive oil
2 small onions, finely sliced
1 lemon, zest and pith removed,
   thinly sliced, plus a few lemon slices
   to garnish
16 sprigs of fresh thyme, plus a few extra
   to garnish

In a small bowl, mix together the wine and lemon juice, then set aside.

Season the chicken breasts with salt and pepper and rub in well. Lightly dust them with some flour, shaking off any excess. With the palm of your hand, flatten the breasts slightly. Heat the olive oil in a large pan. Add the chicken and sear on both sides (some chicken breasts contain water and may spit while cooking—to prevent this, cover the pan with a lid). Once they are well seared and golden brown, remove the chicken breasts from the pan and set aside. Lower the heat, add the onions, season with salt and pepper, and sweat until the onions are soft. Add the lemon slices and thyme and mix well. Return the chicken to the pan, cover, and cook over gentle heat for 3 minutes.

Turn up the heat (but be careful not to burn the onions and lemon), add the wine and lemon juice mixture, then cover and cook for 10–15 seconds, until the mixture is bubbling. Remove the lid and simmer until the liquid has evaporated slightly—the sauce will begin to thicken. Taste and adjust the seasoning if necessary.

Arrange the chicken breasts on a large plate or on individual serving plates and pour the sauce over. Garnish with lemon slices and extra sprigs of thyme.

bocconcini di pollo con aceto alle mele

chicken bites wrapped in pancetta and sage with a cider vinegar dressing

This recipe came out of the blue when I was making a chicken dish for some guests at home. As usual, I had bought too much food and was left with a couple of chicken breasts. In the fridge I found pancetta and fresh sage, so I decided to put these ingredients together with a tangy cider vinegar dressing and made these delicious *bocconcini*, which I served with pre-dinner drinks. They make an excellent appetizer. Alternatively, you can make lots of them in advance for parties or as snacks with drinks. If you serve them cold like this, don't pour the dressing over as they will go soggy. Arrange the *bocconcini* on plates garnished with some salad greens and put the dressing in small bowls for dipping.

serves 6
2 skinless, boneless chicken breasts
6 very thin slices of pancetta, cut in half
12 fresh sage leaves
2 tbsp olive oil
a few salad leaves, to serve
for the dressing:
½ cup/120 ml extra virgin olive oil
¼ cup/60 ml cider vinegar
1 tsp finely chopped fresh parsley
salt and freshly ground black pepper

Cut the chicken breasts lengthways in half and cut each half into 3 chunks. Lay the half slices of pancetta on a clean work surface, place a sage leaf on top of each one, and wrap them around the chicken chunks.

Heat the olive oil in a frying pan over medium heat, add the pancetta-wrapped chicken, and sear all over, taking care not to burn the pancetta. Turn the heat down and, with the help of 2 forks, keep turning the *bocconcini* until the chicken has cooked through. This should take about 10 minutes.

Meanwhile, make the dressing. Place all the ingredients in a small bowl and whisk with a fork until it begins to thicken slightly.

Remove the *bocconcini* from the pan and drain on paper towels to remove excess oil. Arrange on a plate with some salad greens and pour the dressing over. Serve immediately.

petti d'anatra in limoncello
duck breasts in limoncello

Limoncello is a lemon liqueur made on the Amalfi Coast, near my home. When I was a child it used to be homemade only, but now it has become quite an industry and is sold worldwide. It is a very pure liqueur, made solely from lemons, sugar, and alcohol. The citrus/sweet flavor goes very well with duck. Serve this dish with a purée of root vegetables. I like carrot and celery root.

serves 4
4 boneless duck breasts
2 large lemons
1 cup/250 ml limoncello liqueur
salt and freshly ground black pepper
4 tbsp/2 oz/50 g butter
2 tbsp olive oil
To serve
1 lb/450 g celery root, peeled
10½ oz/300 g carrots
large pat of butter

Pat the duck breasts dry and place them in a shallow dish. Peel the lemons with a potato peeler so you get ringlets of lemon zest, then squeeze the juice from them. Scatter the lemon ringlets over the duck, pour over the juice and limoncello, and leave to marinate for about 30 minutes.

Remove the duck from the marinade, dry on paper towels, and season well all over with salt and pepper. Do not discard the marinade.

Clarify the butter in a large frying pan by letting it melt, then when it begins to foam, carefully lifting off the foam with a tablespoon, leaving just the clear, golden liquid. Add the olive oil. When it is hot, place the duck breasts in the pan, skin-side down, and sear well on both sides. Reduce the heat and cook for about 12 minutes, turning the duck over from time to time. This will give you medium-cooked duck, which I think is ideal for this dish. Now turn the heat up to high, pour in the marinade, and let it evaporate, turning the duck over and giving the pan a shake from time to time—this will help the sauce thicken.

Meanwhile, make the purée. Cook the root vegetables in boiling water for 20 minutes. Drain, then pass through a potato ricer, until smooth. Stir in the butter and season with salt and pepper to taste.

As soon as the sauce has thickened, remove the pan from the heat and place the duck breasts on a chopping board. Leave to rest for about 5 minutes, then cut them into slices, arrange on 4 plates or one serving dish, and pour over the sauce. Serve immediately.

petto di faraona ripieno di erbe con salsa al balsamico

breast of guinea fowl stuffed with herbs and served with a balsamic sauce

This is an old recipe from the Naples region, traditionally made with pig's spleen. Spleen is no longer commonly available and probably a little off-putting to a lot of people, so I have used guinea fowl breasts instead. If you prefer, you can use chicken.

serves 4
4 boneless guinea fowl breasts
6 tbsp/90 ml olive oil
⅔ cup/150 ml balsamic vinegar
⅔ cup/150 ml red wine vinegar
1 cup and 2 tbsp/275 ml red wine
salt and freshly ground black pepper
for the stuffing:
1 stick/4 oz/100 g softened butter
4 garlic cloves, squashed and
  finely chopped
1 red chili pepper, finely chopped
¾ cup/2 oz/50 g finely chopped mint
¾ cup/2 oz/50 g finely chopped flat-leaf
  parsley

First make the stuffing. Put all the stuffing ingredients in a bowl and mix together until smooth, adding a little salt to taste. Shape into a ball, wrap in plastic wrap, and put in the fridge until ready to use.

Place the guinea fowl breasts on a chopping board, skin-side down. Make a small pocket in each one with a sharp knife and fill with the herb butter. Fold over the skin from both sides to cover the flesh and secure it with wooden toothpicks, weaving them in and out. Ensure that none of the filling comes out.

Heat the olive oil in a large saucepan, add the guinea fowl breasts, and cook until seared on all sides. Pour in the balsamic vinegar, red wine vinegar, and wine, turn down the heat, and cook for 20 minutes, turning the guinea fowl over halfway through the cooking time. Remove the guinea fowl from the pan and leave to cool. Take the saucepan off the heat and beat with a whisk until the sauce begins to thicken and has an almost creamy consistency. Taste and adjust the seasoning if necessary.

Remove the toothpicks from the guinea fowl and slice. Arrange the slices on a plate and pour the sauce over.

faraona con pancetta e uva passa
guinea fowl with pancetta and raisins

The sweetness of raisins goes well with guinea fowl—although you could substitute chicken if you prefer. You could also buy ready-cut guinea fowl pieces rather than jointing a whole bird, but I do recommend that you use the legs, as they enhance the flavor of the dish. Smoked streaky bacon can be substituted for the pancetta.

serves 4

1 x 2¼ lb/1 kg guinea fowl, jointed into 4 (you could ask your butcher to do this)
generous ½ cup/3 oz/75 g all-purpose flour
¼ cup/60 ml olive oil
4 oz/100 g pancetta, cut into thin strips
10 garlic cloves, unpeeled
1 cup/4 oz/100 g raisins
2 sprigs of fresh rosemary
1 cup/250 ml white wine
1 cup/250 ml chicken stock
salt and freshly ground black pepper

Preheat the oven to 300°F/150°C. Coat the guinea fowl pieces in the flour, shaking off any excess. Heat the olive oil in a large, ovenproof heavy-based pan over medium heat, add the pancetta, and fry until browned. Remove the pancetta from the pan and set aside.

Place the guinea fowl in the pan and cook until seared on all sides. Add the garlic cloves, raisins, rosemary, and wine. Simmer until the wine has reduced by half, then add the stock and return the pancetta to the pan. Cover tightly with a lid, transfer to the oven, and cook for 30–40 minutes, until the guinea fowl is tender. Taste the sauce and add salt and pepper to taste, then serve.

coniglio con aglio e rosmarino servito con bruschetta
rabbit with garlic and rosemary served with bruschetta

Rabbit is cooked all over Italy in different ways and the method I have given here is the way we cook it at home. It was always my son Christopher's favorite dish at Sunday lunches and I dedicate this recipe to him. If you don't like rabbit, you can cook chicken, guinea fowl, or turkey in exactly the same way. Use good extra virgin olive oil for this recipe, since you need quite a lot and the flavor really comes out.

serves 4

1 rabbit, weighing 3 lb 5 oz/1.5 kg, chopped into medium-sized chunks on the bone (including the liver, kidneys, and ribs), or use ready-prepared boneless chunks of rabbit
salt and freshly ground black pepper
all-purpose flour, for dusting
⅔ cup/150 ml extra virgin olive oil
cloves from 1 garlic head, kept whole with skins on
a large bunch of fresh rosemary, broken in half
⅔ cup/150 ml white wine

for the bruschetta:

a few slices of slightly stale bread
a few garlic cloves, peeled but left whole

Season the rabbit with salt and pepper and dust with the flour. Heat the olive oil in a large, heavy-based frying pan. When hot, add the floured rabbit chunks and sear well on all sides until golden brown and quite crisp. Reduce the heat, add the garlic and rosemary, cover with a lid, and cook gently for 30 minutes, turning the pieces of rabbit from time to time. Turn up the heat to high, remove the lid, pour in the wine, and simmer until it has evaporated.

When the rabbit is ready, make the bruschetta. Toast the slices of bread, immediately rub them with the garlic, and then drizzle with some of the olive oil that will have risen to the top of the rabbit sauce. Serve the rabbit accompanied by the bruschetta.

insaccati

preserved meats

Preserved meats are extremely popular throughout Italy, with each region having its own specialties. Although pig is the most common animal from which preserved meats are made, wild boar, goose, and beef are also used.

Bresaola

Bresaola is air-dried beef. It is a popular antipasto on many Italian restaurant menus and can also be found ready-sliced in packages in most supermarkets, although this variety is very "plastic" and tastes nothing like the original. My friend, Mauro Bregoli, who lives in the New Forest, is a master of curing and preserving meat, and his smoked bresaola is exceptional. Whenever I put bresaola on the menu at Passione, I ordered his. The best-quality bresaola can be found at good Italian delicatessens and you should ask for the *punta d'anca*, which is the fleshiest and most succulent part.

Bresaola should be served thinly sliced, drizzled with some extra virgin olive oil and lemon juice, and accompanied with some arugula and shavings of Parmesan cheese or with warm caprino (mild Italian goat cheese).

Cotechino and zampone

These are both a type of huge sausage. Cotechino is a mixture of pork rind, fat, and meat, all ground up and very finely seasoned with spices, then placed inside sausage skins and cooked for a long time. Zampone is pig's trotter ground up with pork rind, back fat, lean meat, and some spices and seasoning. The mixture is then stuffed in sausage skin.

Both are now made commercially and sold in vacuum packs, making them easy to cook in boiling water at home. They are traditionally served at New Year with stewed lentils. The descriptions of both may sound a little off-putting, but I guarantee that if you like sausages, these are the best! They are easily obtainable at Italian delis. Serve with stewed lentils or mashed potatoes and braised cabbage for a filling winter meal.

Prosciutto crudo di Parma

Made from pigs raised in the Emilia Romagna region, this is probably Italy's most renowned cured ham. Other regions have their own versions—for example, San Daniele from Friuli and San Leo from Marche. The best-quality hams are cured on the bone for at least 18–24 months. Prosciutto di Parma is traditionally served as part of an antipasto with other cured meats, pickles, and preserved vegetables (see page 138). See also Antipasto di Pesche e Prosciutto Crudo di Parma on page 98.

Salami

Italy has a vast variety of salami, which are mostly commercially produced nowadays, although many farmers and local *salumerie* still make their own in the old-fashioned way.

Good salami is made with *suino* (pure lard), and the regional varieties have their own flavorings, such as black peppercorns, fennel seeds, chili, and red wine. Some of the most common varieties of salami found in delis abroad are Milano, Napoletano, Felino, Cacciatorino, Soppressata, Finocchiona, and Calabrese, each of which has its own characteristics. I suggest you try a few slices of each before picking your favorite. Serve a selection of salami as part of an antipasto, with pickles and preserved vegetables (see page 138).

Sausages

There is a wide range of Italian sausages available in good delicatessens. Most are pork-based, with flavorings such as fennel seeds, rosemary, sage, and chili. They are usually short and fat, tied with string, and sold loosely from the cold counter. Italian sausages are delicious grilled or fried, as you would cook other sausages, or added to a thick tomato ragu (see page 100) to make a filling pasta sauce.

There is also the luganega sausage, which is a very long pork sausage, common in northern Italy, usually sold by the meter. Buy a long piece and wrap it around in a spiral shape, secure it with toothpicks, and fry it, adding rosemary sprigs and finishing off with red wine. This is delicious eaten with polenta or mashed potatoes.

When I came to England at the end of the 1960s, there were two things I wanted: a pair of Levis and a gun. I had been out hunting with my father on Sunday mornings since I was tiny. Our family had hunted for at least two generations, so it was in my blood. When I was a small boy, I was effectively the dog! I would run through the undergrowth and frighten the birds out. When my father was about to shoot, he would shout, "Hop!," which meant, "Don't move!," and I would duck down. Then we would head back to the village to go to church. My father would leave his gun and pack of game outside. It would be full of blackbirds, wood pigeons, sparrows, and quails.

I remember how strict my father was about his gun. I was never allowed to touch it. He always prepared and stored the cartridges at my grandfather's house and the gun at ours. He frightened me with stories of accidents and injuries, so I was always very careful. He usually let me have a couple of shots with his sixteen-bore at the end of a day's hunting, though.

I bought my gun and Levis almost as soon as I got to England. Then I found there was nowhere to shoot. I spent days going around the countryside asking farmers if I could shoot on their land. Eventually one took pity on me and allowed me on his property, as long as I stuck to wood pigeons and rabbits. There is quite a large hunting fraternity in England, which I was lucky enough to join, and I used to go hunting frequently. These days, if friends ask me to join them, I gladly go along.

verdure

vegetables

Southern Italians love vegetables so much that Neapolitans used to be known as *mangiafoglie*, or leaf-eaters. To this day, Italians have a rich tradition of vegetable cooking and serve vegetables as main course dishes, not just appetizers and accompaniments.

When I was growing up, we usually ate meat only once or twice a week but we enjoyed an excellent, varied diet of seasonal vegetables. Nowadays, we can eat any vegetable all year round, but I miss the anticipation and excitement we felt at the beginning of each new season. We knew we couldn't rely on fresh veggies all year round, so right from the very first crop of spring we would start preserving them for the winter months.

It was a joy eating the vegetables we had preserved from spring and summer—not just for the taste but also for the memories. Every time I opened a new jar, it reminded me of the day I had filled it. It may have been a feast day, or the first day of summer, or even a sad day, but the memories always came flooding back. The taste of those preserved vegetables was out of this world. Preserved eggplants, in particular, were so good that it was a miracle if they made it through to the winter months.

Winter was a joy for me in many ways. I loved the beautiful chestnuts, the dried figs and fruit, and the pungent flavors of preserved summer vegetables. But, after a long winter living on root vegetables and preserved vegetables, spring was really something to look forward to. It brought the first fava beans, peas, zucchini, chicory, cucumbers, onions, asparagus, and endless salads.

The grocery stores gradually came alive with color as they filled with new produce. As spring continued, more and more vegetables arrived—all kinds of cabbages, large eggplants, and tomatoes. Then, with the summer, came an abundance of vegetables and the first fruit crops of the season. It was magnificent. Small pears and figs straight from the trees, herbs, chilies, sweet peppers—everything was available and everything was delicious.

insalata di arancie e finocchio
orange and fennel salad

This salad is typical of Sicily, where oranges are grown in abundance. It is eaten all over the South as well, and I remember it was one of my father's favorite salads as a pre-lunch snack to refresh himself and stimulate his tastebuds—rather like an aperitif. The combination of sweet oranges, the aniseed flavor of the fennel, and the saltiness of the anchovies makes this a very tasty salad indeed.

serves 4

4 oranges, peeled, pith removed
8 black olives, sliced
1 large fennel bulb, finely sliced (reserve the feathery fronds)
8 anchovy fillets
salt and freshly ground black pepper
¼ cup/60 ml extra virgin olive oil
2 tsp red wine vinegar

Take an orange in the palm of your hand and with a small, very sharp knife cut out the segments from between the membranes, discarding the seeds and any pith still attached. Repeat with the remaining oranges.

Place the orange segments and sliced olives in a bowl, then add the fennel and anchovy fillets. Season with salt and pepper (be careful with the salt since the anchovies are already quite salty). Mix in the olive oil and vinegar, leave to marinate for a minute or two and then serve. Decorate with the green feathery leaves from the fennel.

pure di ceci
chickpea purée

Try this purée as an alternative to potatoes or other root vegetables. It makes a wonderful accompaniment to meat dishes, such as Faraona con Pancetta e Uva Passa (see page 115).

serves 4–6

¼ cup/60 ml olive oil
1 celery stalk, finely chopped
½ leek, finely chopped
1 onion, finely chopped
2 small carrots, finely chopped
a few rosemary needles
1¼ cups/9 oz/250 g dried chickpeas, soaked overnight in cold water and then drained
4½ cups/1 liter vegetable stock
salt and freshly ground black pepper

Heat the olive oil in a large saucepan, add the vegetables and rosemary, and sweat until softened. Stir in the chickpeas, then add the stock. Bring to a boil, reduce the heat, then cover the pan and simmer for about 1½ hours, until the chickpeas are tender and have absorbed almost all of the liquid.

Remove from the heat, place in a food processor, and whiz until smooth. Taste and adjust the seasoning. Serve immediately, or make in advance and then heat through gently just before serving.

patate saltate

sautéed potatoes

These are an essential accompaniment to all kinds of meat dishes and roasts. Leave the garlic cloves unpeeled and don't worry about the skin; it all adds to the flavor and appearance of the dish.

serves 4

14 oz/400 g small baby potatoes or fingerlings, scrubbed and cut in half
6 tbsp/90 ml olive oil
3 garlic cloves, unpeeled and squashed with the back of a knife
4 sprigs of fresh rosemary
salt and freshly ground black pepper

Cook the potatoes in boiling salted water until tender, then drain.

Heat the olive oil in a frying pan and add the garlic and rosemary, followed by the potatoes. Allow the potatoes to color on all sides over a fairly high heat, stirring now and again to prevent them sticking to the pan. Season with salt and pepper and serve immediately.

insalata di patate

warm potato salad

For maximum flavor, it is imperative that this dish is served when the potatoes are still warm, so make sure that all the other ingredients are ready as soon as the potatoes are cooked. It makes an ideal accompaniment to Involtini di Pesce Spada con Finocchio (see page 81) for a light al fresco lunch.

serves 4

8 medium baby potatoes or fingerlings
2 medium red onions, very finely sliced
1 teaspoon dried oregano
½ cup/120 ml extra virgin olive oil
3 tbsp red wine vinegar
salt and freshly ground black pepper

Wash and scrub the potatoes well but don't peel them. Bring a saucepan of lightly salted water to a boil and cook the potatoes until tender. Drain and remove the skins, holding the potatoes in a cloth to avoid burning your fingers.

Cut the potatoes into quarters and place in a bowl with all the remaining ingredients. Mix well and serve warm.

tortino di patate e cavolo nero
potato and Tuscan kale bake

Potatoes, cabbage, and Taleggio cheese are a typically northern Italian combination. The climate is much cooler in the North and you would expect to eat such a dish there during winter. I have used Tuscan kale (also called lacinato or dinosaur kale) in this recipe, since I find it much tastier, but you could use Savoy cabbage instead. Tuscan kale is grown mainly in Tuscany and has become widely available in supermarkets. Its name in Italian, *cavolo nero*, means "black cabbage," referring to its long, thin leaves, which are so dark that they look almost black. It certainly stands out from the usual variety of cabbage found in grocery stores.

Taleggio gives the dish a rich, creamy taste but if you can't find it, substitute Fontina or a mature Cheddar.

This is cooked in four individual terracotta dishes, making it an ideal vegetarian main course, served with a simple green salad. Prepare it in advance and then bake once your guests have arrived.

serves 4

1½ lb/675 g Tuscan kale
   (large leaves only)
8 medium potatoes, peeled and
   thinly sliced
1¼ sticks/5 oz/150 g butter
salt and freshly ground black pepper
11 oz/325 g Taleggio cheese, thinly sliced

Remove the stalks and hard central core from the kale leaves and cook in plenty of boiling salted water for 3–5 minutes, until just tender but still slightly crisp. Drain well, rinse in cold water, and then drain again, squeezing out any excess water with your hands. Dry on a dish towel. Cook the potato slices in a saucepan of lightly salted boiling water for 3 minutes, then drain, rinse in cold water, drain again, and dry well on a dish towel.

Preheat the oven to its highest setting. You will need 4 terracotta dishes about 8 in/20 cm in diameter and 1¼ in/3 cm deep (you can substitute one large dish instead if you wish). Grease each dish generously with some of the butter. Arrange half of the potato slices, slightly overlapping, over the bottom of the dishes, dot with some of the butter, and season with salt and pepper. Arrange the kale leaves over the potatoes, with the larger part of the leaf hanging a quarter of the way over the edge of the dish. About 10 leaves should suffice for each

dish. Arrange half of the cheese on top of the cabbage and then season with salt and pepper. Top with the remaining potatoes, then with the remaining cheese. Place a kale leaf in the middle and fold over the excess leaves, pressing gently with your fingers so that none of the other ingredients are visible, then dot with butter.

Cover with aluminum foil, place in the oven, and bake for 25 minutes. Remove from the oven and carefully lift off the foil, taking care not to burn yourself with the steam. Place a plate over each dish and flip over. You should get a lovely layer of golden-brown potatoes on the top. (Serve straight from the dish if you have made a large bake.) Serve immediately.

peperoni ripieni
stuffed baby peppers

For this recipe, try to use baby bell peppers or, if you prefer, the small, sweet long peppers. If you use the latter, slit them lengthways and remove the seeds, then make the filling as below, except for the provolone, which you should slice in strips and place over the top of the peppers. Bake these long peppers for 20 minutes only. If you can't find either type of pepper, use ordinary bell peppers and serve one per person.

serves 4

8 red or yellow baby peppers
2 large potatoes, boiled and mashed
½ cup/3 oz/75 g finely diced provolone cheese
3 tbsp grated Parmesan cheese
1 egg
3 tbsp finely chopped fresh chives
salt and freshly ground black pepper
a little olive oil for drizzling

Preheat the oven to 400°F/200°C. Remove the stalks from the peppers and set aside. With a small, sharp knife, remove the white membrane and seeds from inside the peppers, taking care not to tear the flesh.

Mix together the mashed potatoes, provolone, Parmesan, egg, chives, and some salt and pepper. Using a teaspoon, fill the peppers three-quarters full with the mixture and then put the stalks back in place, like a stopper. Pack the peppers tightly into an ovenproof dish, drizzle with olive oil, and bake for about 30 minutes, until tender. Serve immediately with a good green salad. They are also delicious eaten cold.

agrodolce di peperoni
sweet and sour peppers

Sweet and sour flavors go extremely well with peppers. This dish can be served as an appetizer with lots of bread to mop up the delicious olive oil, or as a side dish to accompany meat and game. It is ideal for making in large quantities for parties, since it can be eaten cold.

serves 2–4

6 tbsp/90 ml extra virgin olive oil
1 large yellow pepper, deseeded and cut into thick strips
1 large red pepper, deseeded and cut into thick strips
3 anchovy fillets
2 garlic cloves, peeled but left whole
6 black olives
1 tbsp capers
1 tbsp sugar
¼ cup/60 ml white wine vinegar
salt and freshly ground black pepper

Heat the olive oil in a large frying pan, add the peppers, and cook until the skins are golden brown. Then add the anchovy fillets, garlic, olives, and capers. Stir in the sugar, then add the vinegar and allow to evaporate. Cook over medium heat for about 5 minutes, or until the peppers are tender. Season to taste and serve either hot or cold.

carciofi ripieni

stuffed globe artichokes

Artichokes are very popular in Italy, especially in the South, where they grow in abundance. In fact, Italy is the largest producer of artichokes in the Mediterranean and a great number are exported as well as eaten locally. Just like chestnut sellers on street corners in cities in the US, we used to have artichoke vendors selling roasted artichokes. The smell was irresistible.

I love artichokes and cook them in a variety of ways—roasted, fried, steamed, and in salads (see page 135). My favorite way of cooking the large globe artichokes is to stuff them and slow-cook them in a pot. Try this recipe; it's simple to prepare, makes a wonderful appetizer, and looks very impressive when served—almost too lovely to eat! When serving, remember to provide finger bowls, spare plates to hold the discarded leaves, and plenty of good bread to soak up the sauce.

serves 4

4 handfuls of fresh parsley, roughly torn
4 garlic cloves, thinly sliced
8 anchovy fillets
16 cherry tomatoes, quartered
4 tsp capers
8 green olives, sliced
4 large globe artichokes
salt and freshly ground black pepper
about 6⅓ cups/1.5 liters vegetable stock
½ cup/120 ml extra virgin olive oil, plus
   a little extra for drizzling

Combine the parsley, garlic, anchovy fillets, tomatoes, capers, and olives in a bowl and set aside.

With a small, sharp knife, remove the bottom outer leaves of each artichoke and cut off the stalk. Trim the base slightly so the bottom sits flat. With your fingers, gently open out the artichoke until you can see the hairy choke. With a small scoop or teaspoon, remove and discard the choke, which is inedible. Season the artichoke cavities with salt and pepper and fill each with the parsley mixture, gently pressing all the ingredients in.

Put the filled artichokes in a large saucepan, then pour in the stock. Pack them in tightly so they don't wobble during cooking. If your pan is too big and there is space between the artichokes, fill the gap with a large potato. The stock should come three-quarters of the way up the artichokes, so if necessary add some more.

Pour 2 tablespoons of olive oil into each stuffed artichoke. Bring to a boil, then reduce the heat, cover the pan, and simmer for 1 hour or until the artichokes are tender; if you can pull out a central leaf easily, they are done.

Carefully lift out the artichokes with a large slotted spoon and place on individual serving plates, then gently open up the artichokes so the filling is exposed. Pour about half a ladleful of the stock over each artichoke and drizzle with some olive oil. Serve immediately, with lots of bread to dip into the sauce.

fagottini di zucchini

stuffed zucchini parcels

This is a different and interesting way of using zucchini. They are simple enough to prepare, but allow yourself some time and you will find that once you get going they are fun to make. They look good, too, and make an ideal appetizer with some salad greens or to serve with drinks. I am sure your guests will be intrigued to know how you got the filling in!

serves 6 as an appetizer

4 large zucchini
1½ cups/12 oz/350 g ricotta cheese
7 oz/200 g potatoes, boiled and mashed
¼ cup/1 oz/25 g freshly grated Parmesan cheese
salt and freshly ground black pepper
8–12 fresh sage leaves
8–12 thin slices of Fontina cheese, about 1½ in/4 cm square (you could substitute mature Cheddar)
a little butter for greasing

With a sharp knife, cut the zucchini lengthways into slices ¼ in/5 mm thick; you should get 4–6 slices from each zucchini. Cook the zucchini slices in plenty of lightly salted boiling water for about 2 minutes, until just tender, then remove and plunge into cold water. Drain and pat dry with paper towels.

Preheat the oven to 475°F/240°C. In a large bowl, mix together the ricotta, mashed potatoes, Parmesan, and some salt and pepper. Take 2 slices of zucchini, place them on a clean, dry surface, and shape them in a cross. Repeat with the rest of the zucchini slices. With your fingers, shape the ricotta mixture into balls about the size of a pingpong ball (one for each zucchini cross). Place a ball in the middle of each cross, place a sage leaf on top, and then fold the strips of zucchini over to make a parcel. Place a slice of Fontina on top and secure with a wooden toothpick.

Line a baking tray with aluminum foil or parchment paper and grease with some butter. Place the zucchini parcels on the baking tray. (At this stage, you can also choose to refrigerate them and cook when needed.) Bake for 10–12 minutes, until golden. Remove the parcels from the oven, place on a serving dish, and remove the toothpicks. Serve warm, with some salad greens.

fette di melanzane con crosta di parmigiano e polenta

eggplant slices with a Parmesan and polenta crust

This idea was given to me by my wife Liz while we were making Involtini di Melanzane alla Parmigiana (see page 134) together. It was her grandmother's version of "vegetarian steak," which she would make for the family during wartime when meat was scarce. It can be served as a snack, side dish or, indeed, a vegetarian main course. The eggplant slices are delicious topped with Salsa alla Crudaiola (see page 142), a little garlic, basil, salt and pepper, or with preserved vegetables (see page 138).

serves 4–6
2 large eggs
salt and freshly ground black pepper
¼ cup/1 oz/25 g freshly grated Parmesan
   cheese
1 large eggplant, peeled and cut
   lengthways into slices ¼ in/5 mm
   thick
all-purpose flour, seasoned with salt and
   pepper, for dusting
1⅔ cups/9 oz/250 g polenta (fine yellow
   cornmeal)
scant ½ cup/100 ml olive oil
fresh basil and sliced cherry tomatoes,
   to serve (optional)

Break the eggs into a bowl, season with salt and pepper, then add the Parmesan and beat well. Dust the eggplant slices in seasoned flour, dip them into the egg mixture, and then coat with the polenta.

Heat the olive oil in a large frying pan and, over a medium-high heat, fry the eggplant slices on both sides until golden brown. Remove, drain on paper towels, and serve either hot or cold, sprinkled with basil and tomato slices, if desired. When eaten hot, they are deliciously crunchy.

verdure alla griglia
grilled vegetables

There is nothing more visually appealing than a plate of mixed grilled vegetables. They can be eaten hot or cold, so can be prepared in advance if necessary. If you have a charcoal grill, then you will obviously get a better flavor. Ideal for barbecues for your vegetarian guests.

serves 4

1 yellow and 1 red pepper, roasted, skinned, and sliced into strips 1¼–1½ in/3–4 cm wide (see page 139)
⅔ cup/150 ml olive oil
1 garlic clove, finely sliced
salt and freshly ground black pepper
2 small zucchini
1 eggplant
1 Spanish onion
12 cherry tomatoes on the vine
a few fresh mint leaves, roughly chopped
a few fresh basil leaves, roughly chopped
balsamic vinegar for drizzling (optional)

Place the roasted pepper slices on a plate and drizzle over a couple of tablespoons of the olive oil. Add the garlic and some salt and pepper and leave to marinate for 15 minutes.

Meanwhile, cut the zucchini and eggplant lengthways into slices about ¼ in/5 mm thick. Score each slice in a criss-cross fashion with a small, sharp knife. Peel the onion and cut it into 4 fairly thick slices. Put the vegetables on a lightly oiled ridged grill pan or under a hot broiler for a couple of minutes on each side, until just tender. Grill the whole tomatoes, too, until soft.

Arrange the vegetable slices and tomatoes on a serving dish, drizzle the remaining olive oil over them, and season with salt and pepper. Sprinkle the mint over the zucchini and the basil over the tomatoes. Arrange the marinated peppers on the dish. Scatter with the garlic, as you wish. You can leave it out, but I prefer it with!

If you like, you can drizzle some balsamic vinegar over the vegetables to give them extra zest.

involtini di melanzane alla parmigiana
baked eggplant rolls filled with mozzarella

This is a specialty from southern Italy, where eggplants are found in abundance and are full of flavor. It makes a wonderful vegetarian main course.

I like making the eggplants into *involtini* (rolls), but if you prefer you can make layers of tomato sauce, eggplant slices, Parmesan cheese, mozzarella, and basil, which is the traditional way of making this dish. Serve with a green salad for an informal mid-week supper.

serves 4–6
1 large eggplant, cut lengthways into
   6 slices about ¼ in/5 mm thick
2 tbsp all-purpose flour
2 eggs, lightly beaten with some
   salt and pepper
olive oil for shallow-frying
salt and freshly ground black pepper
scant ½ cup/1½ oz/40 g freshly grated
   Parmesan cheese
18 large fresh basil leaves
11 oz/300 g mozzarella cheese,
   roughly sliced
for the tomato sauce:
¼ cup/60 ml extra virgin olive oil
1 small onion, finely chopped
14 oz/400 g can of plum tomatoes

To make the tomato sauce, heat the olive oil in a saucepan, add the onion, and sweat until softened. Stir in the tomatoes, season with salt and pepper, then cover the pan with a lid and simmer gently for 25 minutes.

Preheat the oven to 400°F/200°C. Dust the eggplant slices in the flour, then dip them in the beaten egg. In a large frying pan, heat some olive oil to a depth of about ½ in/1 cm, add the eggplant slices, and fry on both sides until golden. Remove and drain on paper towels. Line the eggplant slices up on a large chopping board, season with salt and pepper, then evenly sprinkle 1 oz/25 g of the Parmesan over the top. Place 3 basil leaves on each eggplant slice and top with a couple of slices of mozzarella, reserving half for the topping. Then carefully roll each slice up, making sure they sit seam-side down so they don't unravel.

Line a large ovenproof dish (or individual ones) with some of the tomato sauce and place the eggplant rolls on top, seam-side down. Spoon over the remaining tomato sauce and top with the remaining mozzarrella slices and Parmesan. Place in the oven and bake for 15 minutes, until the top is very lightly colored and beginning to bubble.

insalata di zucchine con menta fresca
zucchini salad with fresh mint

Zucchini are delicious eaten raw, as long as they are firm and fresh and very thinly sliced. This quantity serves two people as an appetizer or four as a side dish. The longer you leave the zucchini to marinate before serving, the better this salad will be. The secret of this dish is to use very fresh zucchini.

serves 2–4
½ cup/120 ml extra virgin olive oil
¼ cup/60 ml balsamic vinegar
1 garlic clove, finely chopped
a handful of fresh mint, finely chopped
salt and freshly ground black pepper
4 small zucchini

In a bowl, whisk the olive oil and vinegar together with the garlic, mint, and some salt and pepper. Trim the ends of the zucchini and, with a potato peeler, slice them lengthways into wafer-thin ribbons. Add to the dressing, mix well, and leave to marinate for 10 minutes or more before serving.

insalata di carciofi, asparagi e finocchio
salad of raw artichokes, asparagus, and fennel

Raw artichokes are surprisingly delicious. They are usually served as a salad with shavings of fresh Parmesan, dressed with extra virgin olive oil and lemon juice. Here, I have omitted the Parmesan and added other crunchy, raw vegetables. If you don't like one of the vegetables, you could replace it with some raw carrots. This makes a lovely, healthy appetizer.

serves 4
4 small fresh artichoke hearts, cleaned (see page 139) and very finely chopped
4 small asparagus spears (use just the tips, about 2 in/5 cm), sliced lengthways in half
2 small fennel bulbs, finely chopped
8 chicory leaves, finely sliced in strips
2 small scallions, finely chopped (optional)
for the dressing:
6 tbsp/90 ml extra virgin olive oil
¼ cup/60 ml lemon juice
salt and freshly ground black pepper

When you have chopped all the vegetables, set them aside and make the dressing. Place all the dressing ingredients in a large bowl and mix well. Add the chopped vegetables and toss together. Serve immediately with some bread.

bietole rosse marinate
marinated beets

Fresh beet doesn't feature much on Italian menus, but I remember it was one of my mother's favorite vegetables, and she would often preserve it. If you follow this recipe, the beets will keep for about two weeks in the oil; if you want it to last longer you can store it in sterilized jars. Once all the beets have been consumed, keep the oil and use it to flavor salads or pasta or to marinate some more beets. You need such a lot of olive oil for this recipe that it's a shame to throw it away.

Serve the marinated beets as you would pickles—perhaps as an antipasto with some salami or air-dried tuna (*mosciame*).

serves 6
1½ lb/650 g raw beets
2 cups/500 ml white or red wine vinegar
8½ cups/2 liters water
a pinch of salt
for the marinade:
2 garlic cloves, sliced
1 tbsp dried oregano
1 red chili pepper, finely chopped
2 cups/500 ml olive oil

Wash and scrub the beets under cold running water. Place them in a saucepan with the vinegar, water, and salt and bring to a boil. Reduce the heat, cover the pan, and simmer for about 1¼ hours, until the beets are tender.

Meanwhile, combine all the marinade ingredients in a bowl and set aside.

Once the beets are cooked, drain them, place them on a clean dish towel or paper towels, and pat dry. Remove the skins with the help of the cloth. Cut into slices, place in the marinade, and mix well. Leave for a day before serving. The beets will keep for several days in a covered container in the fridge, but should be brought to room temperature before serving.

verdure miste sott'olio

mixed preserved vegetables

Preserving vegetables was very common when I was a child. It was a means of enjoying certain vegetables all year round. Nowadays we can get all sorts of vegetables at any time of year, but I still like to preserve them when they are in season. Not only is it an enjoyable task, but preserving gives them a different flavor. Here I have chosen peppers and eggplants, which I have preserved raw so they remain nice and crunchy. Serve with a few slices of prosciutto di Parma and salami, plus lots of good bread for a delicious antipasto.

serves 8–10
1 lb 5 oz/600 g red and yellow peppers
1 lb 5 oz/600 g eggplants
½ cup/5 oz/150 g salt
3½ cups/825 ml white wine vinegar
3 garlic cloves, thinly sliced lengthways
1 red chili pepper, thinly sliced
1 tbsp dried oregano
1 cup/250 ml olive oil

Cut the peppers in half and remove all the seeds and white membrane. Slice lengthways into very fine strips. Peel the eggplants, slice them lengthways, and then cut finely lengthways into strips approximately the same size as the peppers.

Keep the vegetables separate. Take 2 plastic containers, one for the peppers and one for the eggplants. Line one container with the peppers, sprinkle with a good handful of the salt, then carry on with layers of peppers and salt, ending up with salt. Place a weight over the top and set aside. Take the other container and do the same with the eggplants. Leave the vegetables for 1½ hours, after which time they will have exuded a lot of liquid.

Take the vegetables in your hands and squeeze out the excess liquid. Place in separate containers, cover each with the vinegar, and leave for 1½ hours again.

Drain the vegetables, squeezing out the excess liquid with your hands, and place together in a bowl with the garlic, chili, and oregano. Add the olive oil and mix well. Place in a jar, securing tightly with a lid, and leave in the fridge for a couple of days before using. Bring to room temperature before serving.

consigli di gennaro sulla preparazione delle verdure
Gennaro's vegetable cooking tips

Artichokes

To prepare artichokes, remove the bottom outer leaves with a small, sharp knife and cut off the stalk. With your fingers, gently open up the artichoke until you can see the hairy choke. Remove it with a small scoop or teaspoon and discard. If you want to use just the hearts, then remove all the leaves except for a few tender inner ones. If your hands get black while cleaning the artichokes, wash them with lemon juice—the dark stains disappear quickly. Rub the artichokes with lemon juice too, to prevent discoloration and, if not cooking them immediately, keep them in a bowl of water acidulated with lemon juice.

You can cook artichokes in many ways, and even eat them raw when they are young and tender. Simply chop them finely, drizzle with some extra virgin olive oil and lemon juice, then season with salt and pepper. Place on a bed of arugula and top with Parmesan shavings.

Celery

To obtain maximum flavor, bash celery stalks with the flat of a knife blade before chopping them. Use the leaves as well. Added at the end of cooking, they give a wonderful fresh flavor to the dish.

Zucchini

Unless you are using very small, fresh zucchini, the white middle part does not really have much flavor. To make the most of zucchini, cut off the skin in long strips a good ¼ in/5 mm thick and discard the white middle part (save it to add to vegetable stocks). Slice or chop the green strips according to your recipe.

Garlic

Before chopping garlic, squash the cloves whole, skin on, for the best flavor.

Mushrooms

Do not wash mushrooms, whether wild or cultivated. Use a soft brush or slightly damp cloth to clean them. Mushrooms are already full of water and immersing them in more destroys their flavor.

Onions

Soak whole onions in cold water for 30 minutes before peeling. You will find the skin comes off more easily and they will be less pungent when you chop them (so you will be less likely to cry!).

Parsley

Use the stalks, finely chopped, for stocks and soups. They are very flavorsome.

Peppers

To roast peppers, place them under a hot grill, turning several times, until the skin goes black. Remove and leave to cool. Peel off the skin, slice them in half, and remove the white interior and seeds. Then slice according to your recipe.

For a delicious salad, slice roasted peppers into strips, sprinkle with extra virgin olive oil, chopped garlic, salt, and pepper, and leave to marinate for 15 minutes. This makes a good antipasto with lots of bread. Alternatively, to make a sauce for pasta, place the skinned, deseeded roasted peppers in a food processor and whiz with enough extra virgin olive oil to give a smooth sauce. Season, heat through gently, and mix with some cooked penne or tagliatelle.

Potatoes

If you plan to mash your potatoes, don't peel them. Just wash them to get rid of any dirt, then boil them whole. Once tender, drain and remove the skin, which will peel off very easily. You will find that potatoes cooked this way make much better mash, since they are not so watery.

Salads

There are now so many different types of salad dressings from cuisines all over the world—all of them can be delicious, but for me the simple, classic Italian way to dress salads is the best. Place your salad leaves in a large bowl, then sprinkle them abundantly with salt and drizzle with two parts extra virgin olive oil to one part white or red wine vinegar. Mix well, using your hands—you will find that this way the dressing coats each leaf.

Tomatoes

To skin tomatoes, cut a tiny cross in the base of each with a sharp knife. Place them in a bowl of boiling water for no more than 30 seconds, then drain and place in cold water. Peel off the skins.

pomodori

tomatoes

The tomato played a very important role in our culinary life when I was growing up. It is integral to Italian cooking, the basis for so many sauces, and a delight to eat raw in salads.

I remember the anticipation I felt in late summer when I knew my favorite tomato, the San Marzano, was nearly ripe and ready to eat. This long plum tomato grows close to my home, in the Pompeii valley under the shadow of Mount Vesuvius. The fertile volcanic soil helps to produce what I think is the best-tasting tomato in Italy. These tomatoes were perfect in salads and delicious on their own, drizzled with olive oil and sprinkled with salt.

Because tomatoes were so important to our cuisine, we preserved them for use all year round. These days you can buy canned tomatoes in every corner store and supermarket, whole or chopped, plain or herb-flavored. Tomato paste is readily available, and sun-dried tomatoes can be bought at most supermarkets and delicatessens. But when I was a child, we had to prepare the tomatoes ourselves. The hard work made us appreciate the food and brought the family together.

In my house, tomato preservation was a great ceremony and enormous fun. It was usually in September, when the San Marzano tomato was still available, that the family gathered together and the grand procedure began.

We preserved our tomatoes in small beer bottles made of thick, brown glass. The glass had to be thick to survive the pasteurization process. A long wooden table was set out in the yard with lots of chairs arranged around it for all the family to sit at. On the table was a vast supply of freshly cleaned bottles, a bucketful of corks, fresh basil leaves, and kilo upon kilo of washed tomatoes. The tomatoes were cut lengthways into quarters and pushed into the beer bottles along with the odd basil leaf until they were almost full. The bottles were then corked, using a strange gadget. The scene was like a production line, but everyone was cheerful and relaxed, laughing and chatting as they worked.

At the other side of the yard was a large oil drum placed over a tripod. On the bottom of the drum was a raffia sack, folded in two. We placed the filled beer bottles in the drum one by one. Once it was full, water was poured in and another raffia sack placed on top to act as a lid. Then a fire was lit underneath. We took it in turns to sit with the fire all night and make sure it didn't go out until the early hours of the morning, when the process was finished. Once the water had cooled, we removed the beer bottles, dried them, and placed them in pantrys, ready for use in winter.

We always made huge quantities, enough to ensure a year-round supply for us, as well as our family living in the city who could not make their own. The preservation process was perfect. Even when we found a bottle that was a couple of years old at the back of the cupboard, the tomatoes still tasted good. These tomatoes didn't taste like the canned ones you find in the stores; they were something else. There are still families in southern Italy who preserve their tomatoes in this way each year. If I had the time now, I think I would, too.

Besides preserving whole tomatoes, we used to make tomato paste to use throughout the winter months in heavy-based sauces for pasta or meat dishes. The tomatoes were washed and put through a special mincer to extract the pulp. Then the pulp was placed in large, flat, terracotta dishes, covered with nets to keep the flies off and placed on the veranda under the hot August sun for the excess moisture to evaporate.

One member of the family was put in charge of this process. Their duty was to stir the pulp every couple of hours with a large wooden spoon and occasionally sprinkle a few drops of olive oil over the top to prevent a crust forming. The dishes were taken in at night and put out again first thing in the morning. After three or four days, the fresh pulp turned into a thick, delicious concentrate of pure tomato. It was transferred to terracotta jars, drizzled with oil, and sealed with parchment paper and string.

salsa di Pomodoro leggera
light basic tomato sauce

This is the most basic Italian tomato sauce and the most widely used with pasta and other dishes. It's always handy to make a large batch and keep in the fridge—although don't leave it for more than about three days. After this time, it is better to make a fresh batch.

makes enough for 4 servings of pasta
¼ cup/60 ml olive oil
2 garlic cloves, finely chopped
2 x 14 oz/400 g cans of plum tomatoes, chopped
a handful of fresh basil, finely chopped
salt and freshly ground black pepper

Heat the olive oil in a large frying pan, add the garlic, and sweat until softened. Then add the tomatoes and basil, season with salt and pepper, and simmer gently for 25 minutes.

salsa alla crudaiola
fresh tomato sauce

This is a delicious way to flavor summer pasta dishes or to top bruschetta and crostini (see page 155). Alternatively, simply serve it as a salad to accompany fish dishes. Make sure you use ripe cherry tomatoes, good-quality extra virgin olive oil, and lots of fresh basil.

makes enough for 4 servings of pasta
14 oz/400 g cherry tomatoes, cut into quarters
2 garlic cloves, finely chopped (optional)
a handful of fresh basil
6 tbsp/90 ml extra virgin olive oil
salt and freshly ground black pepper

Mix all the ingredients together in a bowl. Leave to marinate for at least 30 minutes. If you don't like garlic, or find 2 cloves too strong, use less or omit it altogether.

If you serve the sauce with pasta you can use it as it is or gently heat it through.

pomodori in bottiglie
"fresh" canned tomato sauce

I call this "fresh" because, although I use canned tomatoes, they are not cooked for very long and are only chopped in half, so when served they look and taste quite fresh. They are almost as good as the tomatoes we used to preserve in beer bottles.

makes enough for 4 servings of pasta

2 x 14 oz/400 g cans of plum tomatoes, chopped in half
12 fresh basil leaves
6 tbsp/90 ml olive oil
3 garlic cloves, cut into thick slices
salt and freshly ground black pepper

Place the tomatoes and their juice in a bowl with half the basil, add some salt and pepper, and mix well. Heat the olive oil in a large saucepan and add the garlic. When the garlic begins to change color, remove the pan from the heat and add the tomato mixture. Place back over the heat and cook gently for 4 minutes, until the mixture is bubbling. Stir in the remaining basil leaves.

Salsa di Pomodoro conposa
heavy-based tomato sauce

This tomato sauce is used to flavor heavy, meat-based pasta dishes such as the traditional Il Ragu (see page 100). You can use it simply as it is if you prefer a heavier tomato sauce. An hour's cooking time should suffice, but if you are cooking pieces of meat in the sauce, you will need about two hours. Remember, the longer you cook this sauce, the richer it will become.

makes enough for 4 servings of pasta

6 tbsp/90 ml olive oil
1 onion, very finely chopped
1 celery stalk, very finely chopped
1 garlic clove, finely chopped
2 x 14 oz/400 g cans of chopped tomatoes
2 tbsp tomato paste, diluted in 1⅔ cups/400 ml lukewarm water
scant ½ cup/100 ml red wine
a handful of fresh basil leaves, torn
salt and freshly ground black pepper

Heat the olive oil in a large saucepan, add the onion, celery, and garlic and sweat until soft. Add the tomatoes, diluted tomato paste, and wine. Season with salt and pepper, add the basil, and stir well. Bring to a boil, then cover the pan—but not completely, so some of the steam can escape—and reduce the heat. Simmer for about 1 hour, until the sauce is thick and silky. Stir from time to time, checking that there is enough moisture; if necessary, add a little more wine or some water.

funghi
mushrooms

I love the changing seasons. My favorite season has always been the autumn. As September arrives, the summer ends. In Minori, that means the tourists leave, the sea becomes rough and populated with different kinds of fish, the weather changes, and there is no more stifling heat. That was always my signal to leave the sea and move to the mountains, where I would lose myself in the forest, picking chestnuts, walnuts, and mushrooms.

The first rain brought life to the changing land. The soil developed a rich, musky smell. Out of the blue, the fruits of the earth appeared. Thousands of mushrooms. There is nothing more magical than a glorious, sunny autumnal morning spent roaming the woods in search of these elusive fungi.

I was introduced to wild herbs and mushrooms at an early age. My mother used to take me with her on her collecting trips in the hills and fields. She showed me what was good to eat, what to try, and what to leave well alone. She collected herbs and mushrooms for her herbal remedies, but we usually came back with such an abundance of produce that she would also use them for cooking.

I was still fairly young when she sent me out on my own to collect mushrooms and herbs for her. Even then, mushrooms intrigued me. I loved trying to distinguish the poisonous ones from the edible ones. It was like a game. I sampled them while I was out and about. Then I thought I was immortal; now I know I was just lucky.

I would take the mushrooms back to my mother. She threw away the ones she thought were poisonous and kept the ones she knew were good. I know so much more about mushrooms now and it breaks my heart to think of the priceless specimens she threw away.

I couldn't believe the abundance of wild herbs and mushrooms in the fields and forests when I moved to England. It was here that my passion grew, and I was determined to become more knowledgeable. I discovered the delights of truffles in England, not Italy—although I am certain they existed in the forests of my childhood, I just wasn't aware of them.

I still go on regular herb and mushroom collecting forays. Some days I come back with seven or eight different edible species of mushroom—pretty ones, ugly ones, colorful ones, big ones, small ones—they are all delicious. On spring days, I like to go out and search for arugula, wild garlic, dandelions, wild fennel, and sorrel.

I love the fact that you can find wild food anywhere—in fields, in parks, by the sea, even on the edge of highways and in city centers.

Remember that although many mushrooms are safe to eat, others are highly poisonous and can be fatal. If you pick your own mushrooms, ensure you can identify them with absolute certainty, or go out with an expert.

funghi misti saltati
sauté of mixed wild mushrooms

This is a simple but truly exquisite recipe, especially after a mushroom hunt when you have lots of different varieties. Nothing is more pleasurable than going into the forest on a clear, crisp, autumnal morning and looking for mushrooms. However, if you are not fortunate enough to go out and pick your own, cultivated ones will suffice if you add dried porcini to give that "wild" flavor. Simply soak ¼ oz/10 g dried porcini in ½ cup/120 ml lukewarm water for an hour, then add them, together with their soaking water, instead of the stock.

This dish is delicious as an appetizer, with lots of bread to mop up the sauce, or as an accompaniment to game or meat dishes.

serves 4
14 oz/400 g mixed wild mushrooms, such as porcini, chanterelles, hedgehog, and wood blewits
6 tbsp/90 ml olive oil
3 garlic cloves, finely chopped lengthways
1 small red chili pepper, roughly chopped
½ cup/120 ml vegetable stock
2 tbsp roughly chopped fresh parsley
salt

Clean the mushrooms with a cloth and brush—do not wash wild mushrooms, as the flavor disappears. Roughly chop any large mushrooms.

Heat the olive oil in a frying pan, add the garlic and chili, and sweat gently until softened—do not let them brown or burn. Turn up the heat a little, add the mushrooms, and stir well for about 1 minute. Then add the stock, keep stirring, and cook for 2 minutes longer, until the liquid has evaporated slightly. Stir in the parsley and salt. Remove from the heat and serve immediately.

funghi sott óliο

preserved mushrooms

Because I am only able to get local wild mushrooms in season, I love to preserve them so I can enjoy them later in the year. In Italy, it is traditional to pick porcini during late summer and autumn and then preserve them to enjoy at Christmas lunch with the antipasto. If you preserve the mushrooms in small jars, they make ideal presents.

serves 10–12

8½ cups/2 liters water
2 cups/500 ml white wine vinegar
1 glass of white wine
1 tbsp salt
2 bunches of fresh rosemary sprigs
3 cloves
2 red onions, cut into quarters
1 red chili pepper, left whole
1 whole garlic bulb, cut in half
4½ lb/2 kg mixed mushrooms (either wild or cultivated), cleaned
4½ cups/1 liter olive oil

Place the water, vinegar, wine, and salt in a large saucepan and bring to a boil. Add the rosemary, cloves, onions, chili, and garlic. Then add the mushrooms, bring back to a boil, and simmer for 5 minutes.

Drain the mushrooms and the other ingredients (onions, garlic, rosemary, and chili) and spread them out on clean dish towels to dry. When they are cold, pick them up carefully with tongs and place in a sterilized ½ gallon/2 kg preserving jar (or several smaller jars). Cover with the oil and leave without the lid on for 2 hours. Ensure that the oil has seeped through to the bottom of the jar, cover with the lid, and store in the fridge for 1 week before eating.

Keep refrigerated and consume within 2 weeks.

cotolette di funghi puffball

puffball cutlets

Puffballs are strange-looking creatures. They are large, white mushrooms resembling footballs and can grow to quite an extraordinary size. They grow wild in fields from the end of August until mid-October and can be found in parts of the North American countryside. If you ever find any, the best way to cook them is to coat them in breadcrumbs and shallow-fry.

They make a hearty breakfast fare with scrambled eggs and bacon, or an Italian appetizer or snack with some preserved vegetables.

serves 2–4

1 medium-sized puffball-weighing about 5 oz/150 g
2 eggs, lightly beaten with some salt and pepper
4 oz/100 g fresh breadcrumbs
olive oil for shallow-frying

Clean the puffball by removing any dirt with a small brush or damp cloth. Cut into slices about ½ in/1.5 cm thick. Dip into the beaten egg, then coat in the breadcrumbs.

Heat some oil in a large frying pan, add the mushroom slices, and fry on both sides until golden brown. Remove and drain on paper towels. Serve hot or cold.

tagliatelle con funghi misti

tagliatelle with mixed mushrooms

If you enjoy making the sauté of wild mushrooms on page 148 and would like to use the same method for a more substantial dish, this is ideal. Fresh or dried tagliatelle are the perfect match for mixed mushrooms. Remember that you can use cultivated mushrooms, adding soaked dried porcini to give that "wild" taste.

serves 4

14 oz/400 g mixed wild mushrooms, such as porcini, chanterelles, hedgehog, and wood blewits
8 oz/225 g fresh or dried tagliatelle
6 tbsp/90 ml olive oil
3 garlic cloves, finely chopped lengthways
1 small red chili pepper, roughly chopped
½ cup/120 ml vegetable stock
2 tbsp roughly chopped fresh parsley
salt
freshly grated Parmesan cheese, to serve (optional)

Clean the mushrooms with a cloth and brush—do not wash wild mushrooms, or the flavor disappears. Roughly chop any large mushrooms.

Place a large saucepan of lightly salted water on the heat and bring to a boil. Add the tagliatelle and cook until *al dente* (fresh pasta will take only about 1 minute; check the instructions on the package for dried).

Heat the olive oil in a frying pan, add the garlic and chili, and sweat gently until softened—do not let them brown or burn. Turn up the heat a little, add the mushrooms, and stir well for about 1 minute. Then add the stock, keep stirring, and cook for 2 minutes longer, until the liquid has evaporated slightly. Stir in the parsley and season to taste with salt.

Drain the pasta and add to the mushroom mixture. Mix well and serve immediately, sprinkled with some Parmesan, if desired.

tramezzini

snacks

Everyone snacks in Italy. Known as *merende* in my day, snacks are part of the fabric of life. Many people only drink a small black coffee before leaving the house in the morning but then stop in a bar on their way to work and buy a croissant or a sandwich. Mid-morning and mid-afternoon, they like to have a little something, quite apart from lunch. There have been *rosticcerie*—shops dedicated to snacks— in Italy for as long as I can remember, and certainly long before fast food became a way of life in Britain and the USA. *Rosticcerie* fall half-way between a restaurant and a coffee bar and sell a whole assortment of delicious nibbles: little pizzas, salami, potato and mozzarella croquettes, endless freshly made sandwiches, hot sausages, and roast quail, all ready to eat.

The Italian equivalent of the doner kebab is a million times more delicious. We love *porchetta*, or spit-roast suckling pig, which is sold from specialist shops and stalls. The succulent slices of pork are served on hunks of rustic bread all over Italy.

All the towns and villages around Minori had a feast day for their patron saint. It was a great excuse to travel all over the region and sample local delicacies. Because there were so many villages scattered over the mountains, there was sure to be a feast day within a few miles every weekend during the summer. Local farmers would bring their produce to sell, housewives prepared the village specialty to serve to visitors, and local shops put on their best displays of gastronomic delights. I would meet up with a gang of friends and we would visit as many as we could reach. We called them *merende* days because we set out to try as many different delicacies as we could find.

spiedini aromatici di mozzarella e acciughe

mozzarella and anchovy skewers

This is a very tasty snack using stale bread, mozzarella, and anchovies. The hot bread is nice and crisp and the anchovies add a tangy taste, making these snacks ideal to serve with pre-dinner drinks.

Use the cheaper mozzarella, such as *fior di latte*, which is ideal for cooking and melting. There is no point using the more expensive buffalo mozzarella, which should only be eaten fresh.

makes 4

12 slices of stale baguette, cut about ½ in/1 cm thick
4 slices of mozzarella cheese
4 tbsp/2 oz/50 g butter
5 anchovy fillets, finely chopped
a few fresh chives, finely chopped
freshly ground black pepper

Preheat the oven to 350°F/180°C. Take 4 wooden skewers and thread 3 slices of bread through the crusts on each one, placing a piece of mozzarella on the middle slice. Put the skewers on a baking sheet and place in the oven for about 10 minutes, until the mozzarella has just melted and the bare slices of bread become crisp.

Meanwhile, make the anchovy sauce. Melt the butter in a small pan, add the anchovy fillets, and mix well.

Pour a little anchovy sauce over each bare slice of bread. Sprinkle chopped chives over the mozzarella, grind over some black pepper, and serve immediately.

bruschetta

bruschetta

Bruschetta is a classic Italian snack that has become increasingly popular in restaurants and pizzerias around the world. I suppose it is Italy's answer to garlic bread. It is very simple to make and is an extremely nutritious snack at any time of day.

1–2 slices of bread per person
slices of stale, leftover bread
   (ciabatta is good)
a few garlic cloves, peeled
salt
abundant extra virgin olive oil
chopped ripe tomatoes (optional)
fresh basil leaves, roughly torn
   (optional)

Toast the bread on both sides, or grill it on a ridged chargrill pan. Remove and immediately rub the garlic cloves over one side of the bread while it is still warm—you will see the garlic melt into the toast. Sprinkle with salt, drizzle with lots of extra virgin olive oil, and top with a few chopped tomatoes and fresh basil, if desired. Serve immediately.

crostini

crostini

Crostini are slices of bread (baguette is ideal) that have been grilled or slowly baked in the oven, then topped with almost anything you like. In Italy, people often serve a selection of crostini as a starter or with pre-dinner drinks. Alternatively, they are a handy way of using up stale bread to serve as a snack instead of the usual sandwich.

Good ideas for toppings include olive tapenade, artichoke paste (both available in good delicatessens), chicken liver pâté (a favorite in Tuscany), a little Salsa alla Crudaiola (see page 142), or a few preserved vegetables (see page 138).

carpaccio di scamorza

carpaccio of smoked mozzarella cheese

I dedicate this recipe to Kate Adie, journalist and war correspondent. While at Passione for dinner one evening, she was talking about the various meals she had eaten around the world and mentioned her favorite Italian dish, which she had had about 20 years ago—a salad of very thinly sliced cheese dressed with raw vegetables and olive oil. She had had this only once, in a restaurant in Bologna, and had never found it on other menus. I quickly went downstairs to the kitchen and recreated the dish. When I took it upstairs, wow, it certainly brought back memories for her!

It's extremely simple to prepare and makes a wonderful light snack or a sophisticated appetizer. You can get hard-smoked scamorza cheese at most good Italian delicatessens. Just remember you will need a good sharp knife, as everything has to be sliced wafer-thin. If you have a mandoline, use that, or the finest slicer on your food processor.

serves 4
2 small scamorza cheeses
½ small shallot, very finely sliced
1 small celery heart, very finely sliced
   (including the leaves)
4 button mushrooms, very finely sliced
freshly ground black pepper
juice of 1 lemon
¼ cup/60 ml extra virgin olive oil

Remove and discard the hard skin from the scamorza and cut them lengthways into extremely thin slices. Don't worry if you don't get a whole slice, as long as the pieces are wafer-thin. Arrange them evenly on serving plates and top with the shallot, celery, and mushrooms. Grind over some black pepper, then drizzle over the lemon juice and olive oil. Leave to marinate for 5–10 minutes and serve with good bread.

crochette di fave

stuffed fava bean cakes

Fava beans are good not only eaten whole, but also when mashed and made into a dough. This recipe takes a little time to prepare but the result is worth the work. The little cakes are delicious hot or cold, or they can be made in advance and reheated in the oven.

makes 36
2½ cups/11 oz/300 g fresh or frozen shelled fava beans
2 cups/9 oz/250 g all-purpose flour
2 eggs
2 oz/50 g butter, softened
1 tsp active-dry yeast, dissolved in 1 tbsp lukewarm water
salt and freshly ground black pepper
olive oil for deep-frying
for the filling:
generous 1 cup/9 oz/250 g ricotta cheese
1 egg
3 tbsp freshly grated Parmesan cheese
3 tbsp fresh chives, finely chopped
a pinch of nutmeg
Blanch the fava beans in a large saucepan of boiling water for 1 minute, then drain well and plunge in cold water. Peel off the skins. Place the beans in a food processor and whiz until mushy. Transfer to a large bowl, add the flour, eggs, butter, yeast mixture, and some salt and pepper, and mix well with your hands to form a smooth dough. Cover with a clean dish towel and leave in a warm place for about 30 minutes, until slightly risen.

Meanwhile, make the filling. Put all the ingredients in a bowl and mix to a smooth paste. Season with salt and pepper.

Shape the dough into balls the size of golf balls. On a lightly floured work surface, roll each ball of dough out into an oval shape about 1/8 in/3 mm thick. Place a tablespoon of the filling on it and roll it up, pinching the edges together to close.

Heat the olive oil in a large, deep saucepan or a deep-fryer. Deep-fry the croquettes, a few at a time, for 2–3 minutes, until golden brown. With a sharp knife, cut in half on the diagonal. Drain on paper towels and serve hot or cold.

pasta fritta
pasta snacks

This is my version of chips! When you make a batch of fresh pasta and have some left over, roll it out, cut it into a taglierini or tagliolini shape, and deep-fry. Flavored with some salt, it makes a fun snack for children or can be served with drinks. You could also flavor it with freshly ground black pepper, a little crushed dried chili, some dried oregano, or anything else you like.

serves 4–6
leftover pasta dough (see page 30)
olive oil for deep-frying
salt

Roll out the dough with a pasta machine to make very thin sheets. Then cut out the thinnest spaghetti shape you have on your machine. As each batch comes out of the machine, roll it into neat nests.

Heat plenty of olive oil in a large saucepan or a deep-fryer. Add the pasta nests a few at a time and fry for about 1 minute, until golden brown. Drain on paper towels. Sprinkle with some salt and serve warm or cold.

The school friends I used to share my merende *with: Gennaro, Alfonso, Franco, Geraldo, and the taller boy at the back is Pepino.*

66 All my friends had nicknames, and they were all called after a food or snack. Alfonso was named Muscione, which means something soft, because when we raided the fig trees in the afternoons he would clamber to the top and feel the figs until he found a soft one. Then there was Sperlungone, named after a long bread, because his mother never made ordinary bread. Hers was always very long, and his roll used to reach from his mouth to his stomach. There was Muzecatella, which means little bite, named because he always took tiny bites of his snack. Biscotti earned his nickname because he liked his snacks very sweet. A very dear friend of mine is nicknamed Melanzana, which means eggplant. In all the years I knew him, he ate an eggplant sandwich every afternoon. A few years ago, someone sent me a postcard of my village. Melanzana was in the background perched on a wall, eating what I would swear was an eggplant baguette.

Lupino got his name from his love of lupinis, a type of bean. To give them their flavor, lupinis used to be dried and put into big cloth sacks, which were then suspended by chains from the cliffs and rocks that overhung the sea. Lupino famously jumped off the rocks armed with his penknife, with the idea of helping himself to an illicit serving of beans. He made tiny little holes in the sacks and filled his swimming trunks with the lupinis. It was a very dangerous mission. The waves crashed against the rocks and he could easily have drowned.

I can remember eating all day long. We certainly weren't starving. We learned about food by talking to the local bakers, butchers, and restaurateurs. We couldn't help but learn about food because the knowledge was all around us. 99

arancini di riso
deep-fried stuffed rice balls

These typically Sicilian snacks are a great way of using up leftover risotto. Traditionally they are filled with different stuffings, such as ground meat or mixed vegetables, and sold as snacks to-go, but to make them simpler you could omit the filling. I have chosen a simple filling of peas and mozzarella. When deep-fried, the mozzarella melts and tastes wonderful as you bit into the *arancino*. I suggest you make lots, since once you start eating them you can't stop!

makes 25
all-purpose flour for dusting
2 eggs, beaten
breadcrumbs for coating
olive oil for deep-frying
for the risotto:
6⅓ cups/1.5 liters vegetable stock
3 tbsp olive oil
1 onion, finely chopped
1½ cups/11 oz/300 g Arborio or other Italian risotto rice
3 tbsp grated Parmesan cheese
salt and freshly ground black pepper
for the filling:
1 tbsp olive oil
1 tbsp finely chopped onion
¾ cup/4 oz/100 g frozen peas
2 tbsp water
3 oz/75 g mozzarella cheese, diced

Make the risotto following the basic recipe on page 58, omitting the butter (or use any leftover risotto you have). Spread the risotto evenly over a baking tray and leave to cool.

Meanwhile, make the filling. Heat the olive oil in a small pan, add the onion, and sweat until soft. Then add the peas, water, and some salt and pepper. Cover with a lid and cook for a few minutes, until the peas are tender. Leave to cool.

Take a little of the risotto and form it into a ball, roughly the same size as a golf ball. You will find it easier if you wet your hands with cold water. Make an indentation in each ball and place a few peas and a couple of cubes of mozzarella in it. Reshape the ball so the filling is in the center and completely covered by the risotto. Dust with a little flour, then coat with beaten egg, and finally coat in breadcrumbs.

Heat plenty of olive oil in a large, deep saucepan or in a deep-fryer. Add the risotto balls a few at a time and fry for 2–3 minutes, until golden brown. Drain on paper towels and serve hot or cold.

la vera pizza napoletana
genuine Neapolitan pizza

You get so many varieties of pizzas these days that I don't blame the Italians for wanting to make it DOC (quality controlled) like wine. Everyone has their own taste and I respect that, but recently I saw chicken tikka pizza on an Indian take-out menu. I do think that this is going a bit far—let's leave pizza to the Italians and chicken tikka to the Indians!

I once had the opportunity of spending some time at the Pizza Academy in Naples, where they are really strict about how the dough is made and what toppings can be used. This is my recipe for the original Neapolitan pizza, which started off as a means of using up the housewife's leftovers: bread dough, tomatoes, cheese, and whatever else they had in their cupboard—which I am sure was not chicken tikka!

makes 2 large pizzas
for the dough:
generous 4 cups/1 lb 2 oz/500 g bread flour, plus extra for dusting
2 tsp salt
¼ oz/10 g fresh yeast (or use 1¾ tsp/5 g active-dry yeast)
1⅔ cups/325 ml lukewarm water
a few dried breadcrumbs or some semolina for sprinkling

for the topping:
1 cup/11 oz/300 g drained canned plum tomatoes
salt and freshly ground black pepper
¼ cup/60 ml extra virgin olive oil, plus extra for drizzling
¼ cup/1 oz/25 g freshly grated Parmesan cheese
a few fresh basil leaves, plus extra to garnish, or dried oregano
5 oz/150 g mozzarella cheese, chopped

Make the dough by putting the flour and salt in a large bowl. Dissolve the yeast in the lukewarm water and gradually add to the flour, mixing well until you obtain a dough. If you find the dough too sticky, just add a little more flour. Shape the dough into a ball and leave to rest, covered with a clean dish towel, for 5 minutes. Knead the dough for 8–10 minutes, until smooth and elastic, then split it in half. Knead each piece for a couple of minutes and then shape into a ball. Sprinkle some flour on a clean cloth and place the dough on it, then cover with a slightly damp cloth. Leave to rise in a warm place for 30 minutes.

Meanwhile, place the tomatoes in a bowl, crush them slightly with a fork, season with salt and pepper, and mix well.

Preheat the oven to 500°F/250°C (if your oven doesn't go this high, just heat it to its highest setting and cook the pizzas for a few minutes longer if necessary).

Sprinkle some flour on a clean work surface and, with your fingers, spread one piece of dough into a circle about 14–16 in/35–40 cm in diameter. Make the dough as thin as a pancake but be careful not to tear it, making the border slightly thicker. Repeat with the other ball of dough, then sprinkle some breadcrumbs or semolina over 2 large, flat baking trays and place the pizza bases on them.

Spread a little of the tomato evenly over each base—not too much, or the pizzas will be soggy. Drizzle with the olive oil, sprinkle with the Parmesan, add a few basil leaves or some oregano, and top with pieces of mozzarella. Place in the hot oven for 7 minutes (a couple of minutes longer if you prefer your pizza crisp). Remove from the oven, drizzle with a little more olive oil, scatter with extra basil leaves, if using, and eat immediately.

frittata di cipolle e porri con crosta di parmigiano
leek and onion omelet rolls in a Parmesan crust

This is a fun and unusual omelet recipe. Once the omelet is cooked, you make a cheese crust by lining a good-quality nonstick frying pan with grated Parmesan and letting it cook until it melts into a whole piece but is still pliable. The omelet is placed over it and the whole thing rolled up like a Swiss roll.

makes 10–12 slices
2 eggs
salt and freshly ground black pepper
2 tbsp olive oil
1 small onion, finely sliced
1 leek, finely sliced (white part only)
½ cup/2 oz/50 g freshly grated Parmesan
   cheese

In a bowl, beat the eggs with a fork and season with salt and pepper. Heat the olive oil in an 8 in/20 cm nonstick frying pan, add the onion and leek, and sweat until softened. Pour in the beaten eggs and cook gently until golden brown underneath. Flip over and cook the other side. Remove from the pan and set aside.

Wipe out the frying pan so it is dry and clean. Place over very low heat and sprinkle the Parmesan evenly over the base. Cook for 1 minute. You will notice the Parmesan sticking together and forming a crust. Gently, with a spatula, lift out the Parmesan crust and place it on a chopping board or a clean work surface. Immediately place the omelet on top, carefully roll it up with the crust, and cut into slices with a sharp knife. It is important to do this quickly or the Parmesan will be too hard to work with.

Either eat straight away or serve cold as part of an antipasto—or take it on a picnic.

66 Not only was I the only boy in the family, I was also extremely skinny when I was young. My mother was determined to build me up, and she went out of her way to bring me *merende* throughout the day. She would embarrass me daily by tracking me down when I was out playing with my friends and calling me over to drink a concoction of freshly beaten eggs and sugar, which she prepared in front of us all. I remember my face burning as I felt my friends watching us.

Another daily ritual was the afternoon snack. But this I shared with my friends. When we met up to play after school, we all carried a paper parcel from our mothers—precious bundles ready for the inevitable moment when all of us were starving. Somehow it was always at five o'clock, and whether we were on the beach, in the mountains, in the village, or the fields, all play would stop. Frantic bartering went on until everyone had the snacks they fancied, then there was a moment of silence. We were like an orchestra. Once we started to eat you could hear a symphony of appreciative "mmms." We even looked like musicians, holding our baguettes carefully as if they were flutes and clarinets.

I learned a great deal about food from these snack sessions, because as soon as we had eaten the first few mouthfuls, stories would begin about where the food came from. "I killed the pig" or "My father milled this flour" and "My mother grew these vegetables" or "I preserved these fruits." We educated each other about food. Many of my childhood friends have since become chefs. I realize now that the quality of those simple afternoon snacks was outstanding. We had bread with all sorts of fillings: pork dripping and sea salt, salami, eggplant, and tomato, mozzarella, and fruit. 99

Mamma, Aunt Alfonsina, my younger sister Adriana, and me, on the balcony at home in Minori.

pane

bread

In Italy, bread forms the basis of every meal. In fact, Italians hold bread in such high esteem that when we want to say that someone is a good person we say they are like a piece of bread (*è come un pezzo di pane*).

At home, my father did most of the cooking but my mother baked the bread. She could easily have bought it, but she insisted on making her own. I felt she was showing us how much she loved us through her baking. She put her heart and soul into it and filled the bread with her happiness as she prepared it for us to eat.

Mamma used a wood-fired oven. She always baked bread on a Thursday and there was a certain purposeful excitement in the way she lit the oven the night before. She cooked the loaves slowly so they would stay fresh all week. In the morning, she would be up at five to stoke the fire. I would hear the crackling of the burning twigs. The smell would slowly waft through the house and infiltrate my dreams. I would wake up hungry, jump out of bed, and run into the smoke-filled kitchen. There I would find three or four beautiful, warm, massive round loaves on the table. The smell was irresistible and it took all my willpower not to grab the bread and tear it apart.

When I make bread now, I put a little bit of my soul into it. Baking bread is the most wonderful part of the working day for me. Early every morning at the restaurant, I spend a couple of hours making the bread for that day. I walk into the cold, empty kitchen before the rest of the world is up. The first thing I do is switch on the oven. Then I take the yeast out of the fridge. To me, it is a living thing to be cared for. It is cold and I can hear it crying out to be fed, so I give it its breakfast. I add the flour, then the water, and watch the big bubbles explode as I mix it together. It gives me such pleasure to watch. Then I leave the dough to rise.

Once it has risen, I take some of the dough and ask it what shape it would like to be today. I tease it into long rolls, round rolls, *filone*, *filoncino*, large *campagnia* loaves—so many gorgeous, voluptuous shapes. The focaccia and filled rolls are made last. I always find something delicious to top my focaccia. Sun-dried tomatoes, olives, onions, and rosemary are favorites. For my rolls I choose the freshest seasonal fillings—such as grilled vegetables, wild garlic, pesto—or mixed cheese and salami.

While the bread is in the oven, I leave the kitchen and go out on to the street for some fresh air. The moment I go back downstairs is magical. The smell of bread baking never fails to overwhelm me with sweet, nostalgic memories of my childhood.

It may sound crazy, but if I bake in the afternoon the bread is never as good. Maybe it is because the ingredients are living things. I think the dough knows from the way I handle it if I'm miserable. In the afternoons I am too tired to put the amount of love into the mixing that I do in the mornings. If I'm happy and energetic, the bread always tastes much better.

The Greek word for bread translates literally as "everything."
I couldn't agree more. I believe bread gives you everything you need.

impasto di pane
basic bread dough

I make most of my dough-based recipes from this basic dough. Bread may seem complicated and an effort to make, but I suggest you try it—there is no more appealing cooking smell than that of your own bread, and certainly no other bread can match the taste. You will find that this bread keeps for days without going moldy. After a day or so it might go hard, but place it in a hot oven for a few minutes and it will taste freshly made again.

makes 2 loaves

7½ cups/2 lb 3 oz/1 kg bread flour, plus extra for dusting
1 tbsp salt
1 oz/25 g fresh yeast (or use 4½ tsp/½ oz/15 g active-dry yeast)
3 cups/700 ml lukewarm water
semolina, polenta, or dried breadcrumbs for sprinkling

In a large bowl, mix the flour and salt together. Dissolve the yeast in the lukewarm water and pour into the flour. Mix well until you obtain a soft but not sticky dough. Turn out onto a lightly floured work surface and knead well for about 5 minutes, until smooth and elastic. Place the dough on a clean dish towel, brush the top with some water to prevent it drying out, then cover with another clean cloth. Leave to rise in a warm place for about 30 minutes or until doubled in size. Knock the risen dough back down and shape it into 2 round loaves. Place on a baking sheet sprinkled with semolina, polenta, or breadcrumbs, cover with a cloth, and leave in a warm place again until doubled in size. Preheat the oven to 475°F/240°C.

Place the loaves on the bottom shelf of the oven and bake for 25 minutes. The way to test if a loaf is ready is to tap it gently on the bottom: if it sounds hollow, it is ready. Remove from the oven and leave to cool. This bread is delicious eaten on the day it is baked. It will keep for about a week and is great sliced and used for bruschetta or crostini (see page 155), toast, or breadcrumbs.

Breadcrumbs Place some sliced stale bread on a baking tray and bake in the oven at 250°F/120°C for about an hour to dry out completely. Remove from the oven and whiz in a food processor. Store in an airtight container.

As a child, I would come running when bread was being made. The smell was so enticing. There is nothing like it.

I loved having bread in the morning. My mother often made me something called a *scodella* from any leftovers. This delicious treat was simply a bowl of bread with milk, sugar, and cinnamon. It was like nectar to a hungry boy.

Every day, we children were packed off with a generous wedge of bread. We would all meet up and search the orchards for ripe fruit to eat with it. My favorite was figs. When they were ready, I found fig trees, climbed to the top with my loaf, and gorged on the ripe fruit. The problem with having a passion for figs was that I was nearly always caught out. The trees gave off milk, which made me sticky and scratchy. It was very difficult to remove—even though I jumped straight into the sea afterwards to try to wash it off.

When the bread was fresh and warm, my little friends and I headed for the village *pasticceria* to have scoops of chocolate ice cream to put into the middle. The result was an inspiration. The memory of the ice cream melting into the warm dough still makes my mouth water.

I was always threatened with a prison diet of bread and water when I misbehaved as a child. It was never much of a deterrent, though, because I loved bread so much that I actually looked forward to the punishment!

Me, dressed as a cowboy, aged 9.

pane rustico

bread with salami, cheese, and eggs

This has to be one of my favorite types of bread. It was traditionally made by farmers' wives as a filling lunch for their husbands while working in the fields, using up all their leftovers of ham, salami, cheese, and even pork fat. I make this bread at Easter time, since the eggs, which are placed around the ring, make it look very pretty and seasonal for Easter Sunday breakfast.

Make sure the eggs are at room temperature; if they are cold they interfere with the rising of the dough. The eggs are cooked in their shells—securing them with strips of dough prevents them exploding in the oven. The eggs come out perfectly cooked and make a delicious addition to this substantial loaf.

makes 1 large ring

4 oz/100 g salami, cut into small cubes
4 oz/100 g pancetta, cut into small cubes
4 oz/100 g prosciutto, cut into small cubes
¾ cup/4 oz/100 g finely diced provolone cheese
¾ cup/4 oz/100 g finely diced Pecorino cheese
1 cup/4 oz/100 g freshly grated Parmesan cheese
2 tbsp coarsely ground black pepper
5 cups/1 lb 5 oz/600 g bread flour, plus extra for dusting
1 tsp salt
1 oz/25 g fresh yeast (or use 4½ tsp/ ½ oz/15 g active-dry yeast)
scant 2 cups/450 ml lukewarm water
semolina or dried breadcrumbs for sprinkling
6 eggs, in their shells

Place all the meat and cheese in a bowl with the pepper, mix well, and set aside.

Mix the flour and salt together in a large bowl. Dissolve the yeast in the lukewarm water and add to the flour. Mix with your hands, gradually incorporating all the flour to form a soft, slightly sticky dough. Turn out on to a floured work surface and knead for about 3 minutes or until smooth, adding more flour to the work surface if necessary. Break off a piece of dough about the size of a tennis ball and set aside. Spread the remaining dough out into a rough circle and add

the meat and cheese mixture, kneading it into the dough until evenly combined. Continue to knead for a couple of minutes, then roll the dough into a large sausage shape about 26 in/65 cm long, and seal the ends together to form a ring.

Sprinkle some semolina or breadcrumbs on a large, flat baking tray and place the ring on it. Make 6 deep incisions around the top of the ring with a sharp knife and with your fingers enlarge each one to make a pocket. Place an egg lying flat in each pocket.

Take the reserved piece of dough, roll it out into a rough square and cut out 12 strips approximately 3 in/7.5 cm long. Place 2 strips criss-cross over each egg, brushing them with a little water so they stick well. Cover the loaf with a clean cloth and leave in a warm place until doubled in size. Meanwhile, preheat the oven to 425°F/220°C.

Bake the loaf for 30 minutes or until golden. This is delicious served hot or cold.

focaccia con aglio e rosmarino
focaccia with garlic and rosemary

I remember having focaccia as a child, although we did not know it by that name. We would flatten leftover bread dough and drizzle it with extra virgin olive oil and sea salt. This would often be my breakfast. When I became a chef, I discovered that this simple bread was commonly known as focaccia, and during my many travels over Italy I saw it being made in different ways with various toppings and even stuffed. I used to bring these ideas back to my restaurant and develop them further.

You can top focaccia with almost anything you like—cherry tomatoes, olives, grilled vegetables, herbs, but always with extra virgin olive oil and sea salt. In this basic recipe, I have given you just a few simple ingredients—garlic, rosemary, oil, and sea salt—which together make a delicious topping. Focaccia is best served warm straight from the oven, but if you make it in advance you can always reheat it in a hot oven for a few minutes just before serving. It makes an ideal accompaniment to meals instead of bread rolls, and can even be sliced in half and filled with some ham and cheese to make a substantial sandwich.

makes 1 loaf
for the dough:
generous 4 cups/1 lb 2 oz/500 g bread flour
2 tsp salt
½ oz/15 g fresh yeast (or use 2 heaped tsp/¼ oz/10 g active-dry yeast)
1½ cups/350 ml lukewarm water
semolina or polenta for sprinkling
for the topping:
2 tbsp extra virgin olive oil, plus extra for drizzling
2 large garlic cloves, finely chopped
needles from 3 fresh rosemary sprigs, finely chopped
1 tsp flaky sea salt, preferably Maldon
freshly ground black pepper

Preheat the oven to 475°F/240°C. Make the dough in the same way as the Basic Bread Dough (see page 172). You will need a baking tray about 15 x 11 in/37.5 x 27.5 cm. After the first rising, place the dough on a lightly floured work surface and roll out into a rectangular shape roughly the size of the baking tray. Warm the baking tray in the hot oven for about 10 seconds, then remove and sprinkle with semolina or polenta.

Place the rolled-out dough on the tray and pour the olive oil on to the dough. With your fingers, spread the oil all over the dough. Leave for 5 minutes, then poke the dough all over with your fingers to make indentations. Sprinkle the garlic and rosemary over the top, followed by the salt and pepper. Leave to rest in a warm place for 30 minutes (a good place is on the stovetop, if it is directly above the oven).

Bake for about 15 minutes, until evenly golden brown. Check the focaccia from time to time, since domestic ovens often color one side and not the other, so turn the baking tray around accordingly. Once cooked, remove from the oven and immediately drizzle some olive oil all over. Leave to cool, then cut into squares.

This bread is delicious eaten on the day it is baked, but it will keep for a few days, and you can freshen it up in the oven for a few minutes just before serving.

panini con verdure alla griglia e parmigiano
mixed grilled vegetable and Parmesan rolls

This is an excellent way to use up leftovers. I have suggested grilled vegetables here, but you can also use ham, salami, cheese, even pesto (see page 44). The rolls look good and are very tasty—great for taking on picnics or adding to your bread basket.

makes about 18
for the dough:
generous 4 cups/1 lb 2 oz/500 g bread
    flour, plus extra for dusting
2 tsp salt
½ oz/15 g fresh yeast (or use 2 heaped
    tsp/¼ oz/10 g active-dry yeast)
1½ cups/350 ml lukewarm water
semolina or coarse polenta for
    sprinkling
extra virgin olive oil for drizzling
for the filling:
2 tbsp olive oil
3 tbsp freshly grated Parmesan cheese
    (or Cheddar, if you prefer)
1 large zucchini, cut into strips
    and grilled
1 eggplant, cut into strips and grilled
1 yellow and 1 red pepper, roasted and
    cut into strips (see page 139)
salt and freshly ground black pepper
a handful of cherry tomatoes (optional)

Make the dough in the same way as the Basic Bread Dough (see page 172). After the first rising, place it on a lightly floured work surface and roll out into a rectangle about ⅛ in/3 mm thick. Drizzle with the olive oil and sprinkle the cheese all over. Cover with the grilled vegetables and season with salt and pepper. Gently roll up lengthways like a Swiss roll, tucking in any filling that escapes at either end.

With a sharp knife, slice into rolls about 1¼ in/3 cm wide. Sprinkle some semolina or polenta on a baking tray and place the rolls on it. Place a tomato on a few of the rolls, if desired. Leave to rest for 20 minutes.

Meanwhile, preheat the oven to 475°F/ 240°C. Bake the rolls on the top shelf of the oven for 12 minutes or until golden brown. Remove from the oven and immediately drizzle with extra virgin olive oil.

schiacciata della vendemmia

sweet tart with harvest grapes

At harvest time in Italy it is traditional to put aside some grapes to consume over Christmas. They become deliciously sweet and squashy and make a perfect filling for a pie. I am not suggesting you preserve grapes for this recipe, as nowadays you find them all year round. Use the sweet varieties, such as Muscatel. Don't be alarmed by the large quantity of cinnamon—the taste is not at all overpowering.

serves 4–6

¾ oz/20 g fresh yeast (or use 3½ tsp/
 ⅓ oz/10 g active-dry yeast)
⅔ cup/150 ml lukewarm water
scant 2½ cups/10½ oz/300 g bread flour,
 plus extra for dusting
1 tsp salt
dried breadcrumbs, polenta, or semolina
 for sprinkling
1 lb/450 g white or black grapes
 (or a mixture)
⅓ cup/75 ml extra virgin olive oil
⅓ cup/2½ oz/65 g sugar
1 tbsp ground cinnamon
a bunch of fresh rosemary,
 plus a few sprigs to decorate
confectioner's sugar for dusting

Dissolve the yeast in the lukewarm water and set aside. Sift the flour into a large bowl, mix in the salt, and make a well in the center. Gradually pour in the yeast mixture, mixing it with the flour to make a soft but not sticky dough. Turn out and knead on a lightly floured surface for about 10 minutes, until smooth and elastic. Divide the dough into 2 balls, cover with a clean dish towel, and leave to rest for 5 minutes.

Preheat the oven to 400°F/200°C. Roll out one of the balls of dough into a round about ¹/₁₂ in/2 mm thick and 6 in/15 cm in diameter. Sprinkle a large baking tray with breadcrumbs, polenta, or semolina then lift the dough on to it. Set aside a small bunch of 8–10 grapes and arrange the rest over the dough, leaving a border of about 1 in/2.5 cm all around. Drizzle with 3 tablespoons of the olive oil, sprinkle with ¼ cup/2 oz/50 g of the sugar, and all of the cinnamon. Then sprinkle over the rosemary needles.

Roll out the other half of dough to the same size and place this over the filling, pressing down the edges well. Trim away any excess and crimp the edges with your fingers so that the pie is well sealed. Drizzle the remaining olive oil over the top and sprinkle with the remaining sugar. Place in the oven and bake for 10 minutes, then place the reserved grapes on top with a few sprigs of rosemary. Bake for a further 10 minutes until pale gold and lightly caramelized. Dust with confectioner's sugar and serve warm.

dolci

desserts

I have a very sweet tooth and adore sweets and cakes. When
I make them, I use traditional methods to try to recapture the tastes
of my childhood. I like to create rustic desserts flavored with sweet
spices such as cinnamon.

It would be no exaggeration to say that I have spent my whole life
working with food. I earned my first wages at the local *pasticceria*,
which was owned by the father of a good friend of mine. He was
exactly as you would imagine the owner of a cake shop to be, with a
chubby, smiling face and a big belly from eating too many of his own
cakes. When I went over to my friend's house, I was always given a
job to do—usually skinning almonds. Not the nicest job in the world
but it paid good money—enough to fund my trips to the cinema.

The almonds were gathered from just outside Minori. Sacks full of
them were brought down from the mountains and put outside in the
sun to dry. The nuts were cracked and shelled, then given to me to
peel—one by one. I was equipped with two buckets of water, one hot
and one cold. I had to soak the almonds in the hot water, take them
out, peel them, and then drop them into the cold. I ate as many as I
returned to the shop, but a blind eye was turned.

It was a wonderful cake shop. When I passed it in the morning, the
smell of baking was good enough to stop you in your tracks. Italy still
has good *pasticcerie* but the local, seasonal element has disappeared.
My friend's father used fresh eggs, freshly milled flour from the
village mill, and fruit from local orchards. He baked for the shop
every day: all kinds of pastries, local specialty cookies, sponge cakes,
jam tarts, chocolate cake, and ice cream. Everyone in the village loved
him, and he was often requested to make special cakes for weddings,
parties, and feasts. People would come in with their own recipes or
bring in their own spices to be added to their cakes. He would nod
and smile and agree to their wishes, but I knew that he never really
stuck to the recipes he was given, and generally added a few spices
of his own. He always produced a masterpiece and the ladies of the
village adored him for it.

I was very lucky in my choice of friends. One of them, Antonio, had a father who owned a coffee shop in the village. It sold all sorts of things besides coffee, and the house specialty was a beautiful lemon sorbet. He made it from a huge block of ice, plus sugar, lemon juice, and zest—nothing else. A big aluminum spoon slowly turned the ice, mixing in the other ingredients until it was smooth and sweet like a cream. You could smell the lemons from a quarter-mile away.

It was Antonio's job to zest the lemons and he was always made to do this before he could come and play with me. If I was in need of a playmate, I helped him out. We would sit together grating the lemons for the zest and then squeezing out the juice. Of course, I did have an ulterior motive: his father would give us a big portion of sorbet with honey on top when we were done. I learned to make sorbet from this man. Not long ago, I returned to Italy and went to see him. He is very old now but he remembered me. "Gennarino," he said (which is what he called me all those years ago; it means little Gennaro), "do you remember the lemons?"

Crostata di Limone

Amalfi lemon tart

This delicious lemon tart is made with puff pastry instead of the traditional shortcrust, and the store-bought variety is absolutely fine (unless you enjoy making your own puff pastry, which is quite a lengthy procedure). I normally make this tart with lemons from the Amalfi Coast, which have a wonderful aroma; however, they are not easy to source so get the best unwaxed organic variety that you can find. Simple to prepare, this lemon tart makes a lovely dessert at any time.

Serves 6–8

scant ½ cup/100 ml water
1 tbsp sugar
peel of 2 Amalfi lemons, cut into
    julienne (thin strips)
10½ oz/300 g puff pastry
    (all-butter is best)

for the filling:

3 eggs, separated
1 cup/7 oz/200 g sugar
zest and juice of 2 Amalfi lemons
2 tbsp/1 oz/25 g butter, melted,
    plus extra for greasing
1 cup/8 oz/225 g ricotta cheese, sieved
3 tbsp all-purpose flour, plus extra for
    dusting and rolling

Preheat the oven to 375°F/190°C.

To remove the bitterness from the lemon strips, place the water and sugar in a small saucepan over medium heat and stir until the sugar has dissolved. Stir in the lemon strips, increase the heat, and bring to a boil. Reduce the heat and simmer for 2 minutes. Drain, discard the liquid, dry the lemon strips on paper towels, and leave to cool.

Lightly grease a 10 in/25 cm loose-bottomed tart pan with a little butter and dust lightly with some flour. On a lightly floured work surface, roll out the puff pastry to a round about ¼ in/5 mm thick. Line the prepared pan with the pastry, making sure it comes slightly over the edge. Line the pastry with parchment paper, fill with pie weights, dried beans, or rice and blind bake for 15 minutes; after 10 minutes, remove the weights and continue to bake until the pastry is golden. Remove from the oven and set aside.

Reduce the oven to 275°F/130°C.

To make the filling, beat the egg yolks and sugar together until light and fluffy and doubled in volume—an electric mixer is best for this. Add the lemon zest and juice and melted butter, and mix well. Stir in the ricotta and sift in the flour. Whisk well to remove any lumps.

In another bowl, whisk the egg whites until stiffened, then fold carefully into the ricotta mixture until well incorporated. Pour into the pastry base and bake for 45–50 minutes until set. About 15 minutes before the end of cooking time, arrange the lemon strips over the top and continue to bake.

Remove from the oven and allow to cool. Gently remove the tart from the pan and transfer to a plate to serve.

frutta cotta

dried fruit compote with rum

You can buy a wonderful array of dried fruit in supermarkets and healthfood shops and liven it up with spices and rum. This is so simple to prepare that it is worth making a large batch and storing it in sterilized airtight jars. It will keep for a couple of months. Serve with some mascarpone or whipped cream for a delicious, warming winter dessert.

serves 6–8
grated zest and juice of 1 lemon
grated zest and juice of 1 orange
2 sprigs of fresh rosemary
1 cinnamon stick
6 cloves
½ tsp fennel seeds
½ tsp black peppercorns
2½ cups/1 lb 2 oz/500 g sugar
2 cups/500 ml water
2¼ lb/1 kg mixed dried fruit, such as prunes, apricots, figs, raisins, apples, pears, and peaches
scant 1 cup/200 ml dark rum

Put the citrus zest and juice, rosemary, cinnamon, cloves, fennel seeds, peppercorns, sugar, and water in a large saucepan and bring to a boil, stirring occasionally to dissolve the sugar. Reduce the heat, cover the pan, and simmer gently for 5 minutes. Add the hardest fruit, such as prunes, first and simmer for 3 minutes, then add the rest of the fruit and simmer for 5 minutes.

Remove from the heat and add the rum. Stir well and leave to stand, covered, for at least a day before use. Heat through gently before serving.

fragole fresche con salsa di fragole

fresh strawberries with strawberry sauce

For a simple summer dessert with minimum effort but maximum taste, this is ideal. If you like, you can serve it with good-quality vanilla ice cream.

serves 4

1 lb/450 g strawberries, cut into quarters
sprigs of fresh mint and confectioner's
   sugar, to decorate (optional)

for the sauce:

1½ tbsp/¾ oz/20 g butter
⅓ cup/2½ oz/65 g sugar
¼ lemon
7 oz/200 g strawberries, cut in half

First make the sauce. Put the butter and sugar in a saucepan and place over a gentle heat. Spear the lemon quarter with a fork and use it to stir the butter and sugar until the butter has melted and the sugar has dissolved. Press the lemon with the fork to squeeze out all the juice, then discard it. Stir in the halved strawberries, then remove from the heat and push the mixture through a sieve. Leave to cool.

Pour the sauce on 4 serving plates, then top with the fresh strawberries. Decorate with sprigs of mint and sprinkle with confectioner's sugar, if desired.

gelato passione
limoncello and strawberry ice cream

This recipe was devised by my friend Albino Barberis who makes the best ice cream this side of Milan. He came up with the idea when we opened Passione, combining limoncello liqueur, which comes from the Amalfi Coast, with wild strawberries because of my fascination for wild food. The result was outstanding and it has become a firm favorite on our dessert menu. I make it with cultivated strawberries, but if you want to treat yourself to wild strawberries, then even better!

serves 6–8
9 oz/250 g strawberries
3 egg yolks
⅓ cup/2½ oz/65 g superfine sugar
1¼ cups/300 ml heavy cream
⅔ cup/150 ml whole milk
1 cup/250 ml limoncello liqueur
grated zest of ½ lemon

Put a large plastic container in the freezer ready for the ice cream. Slice half the strawberries quite thinly and set aside. Blend the remaining strawberries in a blender or food processor to a purée. Set aside.

Beat together the egg yolks and sugar in a bowl. Put the cream and milk in a saucepan and bring gently to a boil. As it begins to boil, remove from the heat and beat in the egg mixture. Return to a low heat and cook for about 1 minute, stirring all the time with a wooden spoon, until slightly thickened. Remove from the heat and fold in the sliced and puréed strawberries. Then stir in the limoncello and lemon zest. Remove the container from the freezer and pour in the mixture until it is about three-quarters full (if you have extra mixture, pour it into another plastic container). Leave to cool, then place, uncovered, in the freezer.

After 30 minutes, remove and stir well, then replace in the freezer. Leave for another 30 minutes and repeat the procedure a few times until the ice cream is frozen. Alternatively, if you have an ice cream machine, churn the ice cream until it thickens, then place in a container in the freezer.

semifreddo di mandorle e cioccolato bianco
semifreddo of almonds and white chocolate

Semifreddo is a classic Italian dessert that is served straight from the freezer but does not set as firm as ice cream. It is ideal for the warmer months and can be made in advance and kept in the freezer until you need it. I have used individual baba molds here but you could use ramekins or one large mold, such as a loaf pan, and serve it sliced.

serves 6
3 egg yolks
6 tbsp/3 oz/75 g sugar
3 oz/75 g white chocolate, finely
   chopped
1 cup and 2 tbsp/275 ml whipping cream
for the *croccante* (praline):
3 tbsp caster sugar
1 cup/5¹/₃ oz/150 g blanched almonds,
   roughly chopped
4½ tbsp/65 ml water

First make the *croccante*. Place the sugar in a small, heavy-based pan over medium heat and stir with a wooden spoon until it begins to caramelize and turn golden brown. At this stage, add the almonds and water and mix well. Remove from the heat, pour the mixture on to a lightly oiled baking tray or marble board, and leave to cool.

Whisk the egg yolks and sugar together in a bowl until light and fluffy and increased in volume. Break up the cooled *croccante* quite roughly and add about two thirds of it to the egg mixture, together with the white chocolate. Set the remaining *croccante* aside, to decorate.

In a separate bowl, whip the cream to stiff peaks, then fold it into the mixture. Line six 3½ in/9 cm baba molds or ramekins with plastic wrap, fill them with the mixture, and place in the freezer for at least 2 hours, until frozen. To serve, remove from the freezer and leave at room temperature for a few minutes, then turn out on to plates and peel off the plastic wrap. Sprinkle with the reserved *croccante*, if desired.

panna cotta con menta fresca

fresh mint panna cotta drizzled with honey

Panna cotta literally translated means "cooked cream" and that's basically what it is. You can try all sorts of different flavorings—this one is especially light and subtle with the cool, fresh mint. It's a very simple dessert to make, and it should be prepared in advance to give it time to set. I find it sets best if you make it the night before. It will keep for 3–4 days in the fridge.

serves 4

1 cup/250 ml heavy cream
1 cup/250 ml milk
1½ tbsp sugar
10 fresh mint leaves, finely chopped
a couple of drops of vanilla extract
1 tbsp/¼ oz/8 g unflavored gelatin
   powder
¼ cup/60 ml clear honey
a few dark chocolate shavings (optional)

Put the cream, milk, sugar, mint, and vanilla in a small saucepan and bring gently to a boil. As soon as it begins to bubble, remove from the heat, cover with a lid, and leave to rest for 5 minutes. This is done to allow the mint to infuse. Strain the cream through a fine sieve and discard the mint.

Add the gelatine to the hot cream mixture and stir well, making sure that the gelatine dissolves. The mixture will take on an oily appearance—don't worry, this is because of the gelatine and is quite normal. Pour the mixture into 4 ramekins or baba molds and place immediately in the fridge. Leave for at least 4 hours, until set.

To serve, run a knife around the edge of each panna cotta and then turn the mold upside down on to an individual serving dish to tip it out. Drizzle some clear honey on top and scatter with a few chocolate shavings, if desired. If using ramekins, you don't have to tip the panna cotta out if you don't want to; just drizzle the honey on top and serve in the ramekins.

pastiera di grano
Neapolitan Easter wheat and ricotta tart

This dessert is believed to date back to pagan times, when Neapolitans would offer all the fruits of their land to the mermaid, Partenope, in spring: eggs for fertility, wheat from the land, ricotta from the shepherds, the aroma of orange flowers, vanilla to symbolize faraway countries, and sugar in honor of the sweet mermaid. It is said that the mermaid would take all these ingredients, immerse herself in the sea of the Bay of Naples, and give back to the Neapolitans a dessert that symbolized fertility and rebirth. The recipe as we know it today came from Neapolitan convents, and nuns would make it for rich nobles of the area.

My mother and aunts would always make it at Easter. It is still made today, at home as well as in pastry shops throughout the Campania region. In Naples, Easter wouldn't be Easter without a *Pastiera di Grano*. Wheat sounds like a strange ingredient for a tart but it really is delicious, especially with the delicate flavor of orange blossom water. *Grano cotto* (pre-cooked wheat) is sold in cans or jars in Italian delicatessens, and orange blossom water can be found in supermarkets.

serves 12

14 oz/400 g can of *grano cotto* (pre-cooked whole wheat berries)
½ cup/120 ml milk
½ tsp vanilla extract
generous 1 cup/9 oz/250 g ricotta cheese
5 egg yolks
2 cups/7 oz/200 g confectioner's sugar, plus extra for decorating
4½ oz/120 g mixed candied peel, finely chopped
1½ tbsp orange blossom water
grated zest of ½ orange
2 egg whites

for the sweet shortcrust pastry:

3¼ cups/14 oz/400 g all-purpose flour
3 eggs
½ cup/4 oz/100 g superfine sugar
1¼ sticks/5 oz/150 g butter, at room temperature, diced
grated zest of 1 lemon

First make the pastry. Sift the flour onto a work surface and make a well in the center. Add the eggs, sugar, butter, and half the lemon zest (reserve the rest for the filling) and lightly blend everything together with your fingertips until you have a smooth dough. Wrap in plastic wrap, chill for 1 hour, then roll out thinly and use to line a 10 in/25 cm loose-bottomed tart pan, trimming the excess. Place in the fridge until ready to use. Do not discard the pastry trimmings; shape them into a ball, wrap in plastic wrap, and place in the fridge.

Preheat the oven to 325°F/170°C. Place the wheat, milk, 1 tablespoon of the remaining lemon zest, and the vanilla extract in a small saucepan, mix well, and bring to a boil. Reduce the heat and simmer gently until the wheat has absorbed all the liquid. Remove from the heat and leave to cool.

Mash the ricotta with a fork and beat in the egg yolks until light and fluffy. Sift in the confectioner's sugar and beat until well incorporated, then beat in the candied peel, orange blossom water, the remaining lemon zest, and the orange zest. Stir in the cooled wheat mixture.

In a separate bowl, whisk the egg whites until stiff. Then fold carefully but thoroughly into the ricotta and wheat mixture.

Remove the pastry base from the fridge and pour in the mixture. Roll out the remaining pastry quite thinly and cut it into 1 in/2.5 cm strips, roughly the length of the tart pan. Arrange the strips criss-cross over the tart roughly 1 in/2.5 cm apart, trimming off any excess and pressing the ends against the edge of the pastry base to seal. Place in the oven and bake for 50 minutes, until lightly browned but still moist. Leave to cool, then sift over some confectioner's sugar to decorate.

torta al cioccolato e vino rosso
chocolate and red wine cake

Chocolate and red wine go well together, so what better way to combine them than in a cake? This cake is light, moist, and simple to prepare. For a special occasion, coat with chocolate sauce (see below) and decorate with chocolate shavings and a sprig of flowering rosemary.

makes an 8 in/20 cm cake
1¾ sticks/7 oz/200 g butter, softened
1¼ cups/9 oz/250 g sugar
4 eggs, beaten
¼ cup/1 oz/25 g unsweetened cocoa powder
2 cups/9 oz/250 g all-purpose flour
1 tsp baking powder
½ tsp ground cinnamon (optional)
scant ½ cup/100 ml red wine
½ tsp vanilla extract
generous ½ cup/5 oz/150 g dark
    chocolate chips
chocolate sauce and shavings, to decorate

Preheat the oven to 350°F/180°C and lightly grease a loose-bottomed 8 in/20 cm cake pan.

Cream the butter and sugar together in a bowl, until light and fluffy. Gradually beat in the eggs. Then sift in the cocoa, flour, baking powder, and cinnamon if using, and fold in. Mix in the red wine and vanilla, then fold in the chocolate.

Pour the mixture into the prepared cake pan and bake for 1 hour, until a skewer inserted in the center comes out clean. Remove from the oven and allow to cool in the pan, then carefully turn out. Coat with the chocolate sauce below and chocolate shavings, if desired.

salsa al cioccolato
chocolate sauce

This lovely, rich chocolate sauce is ideal for covering cakes, since when cooled it sets, and goes quite hard. It can also be used to pour over ice cream or panna cotta (see page 192). In both cases, use immediately after making, before it has a chance to set. If necessary, make a large batch and keep it for up to a week in the fridge; just place whatever quantity you need in a bowl set over a pan of hot water to melt before using.

makes enough to cover two cakes
½ cup/120 ml light cream
5 oz/150 g dark chocolate, broken up
1½ tsp cocoa powder
1½ tsp glucose syrup
2 tbsp/1 oz/25 g butter
1 tbsp sugar

Place all the ingredients in a bowl set over a saucepan of hot water (make sure the bowl does not touch the water) and stir constantly until the chocolate has melted and the sauce has a smooth, silky consistency. Pour through a sieve, if necessary, to strain out any lumps of cocoa. Leave to cool slightly (only 1–2 minutes) before using to decorate the cake (above) or as you wish.

torta alle pere

pear cake

This cake is deliciously moist and can be served either as a dessert or at teatime. Use Bartlett pears for best results. The glaze is simple to make but you could always do without it—it doesn't really affect the taste of the cake but just gives it a nice, shiny glow!

makes a 10 in/25 cm cake

2 eggs

1 egg yolk

¾ cup/5 oz/150 g sugar

4 tbsp/2 oz/50 g butter, cut into small chunks, plus extra for greasing

1 tbsp clear honey

3 tbsp whole milk

1 cup and 2 tbsp/5 oz/150 g all-purpose flour

1 tsp baking powder

a pinch of salt

1 tsp vanilla extract

5 pears

¼ cup/60 ml apricot jam, to glaze (optional)

Preheat the oven to 350°F/180°C. Lightly grease a 10 in/25 cm round shallow cake pan with butter and line the base with a circle of parchment paper.

In a bowl, beat the eggs, egg yolk, sugar, butter, and honey together until light and fluffy. You will find this easier and quicker with an electric mixer. Gradually add the milk, beating well. Then sift the flour, baking powder, and salt over the top and fold in with a metal spoon. Add the vanilla and mix. Core and dice 3 of the pears and mix them in.

Pour the mixture into the prepared cake pan. Core and thinly slice the 2 remaining pears and arrange them on top. Bake for 45 minutes, until the cake is risen and golden brown. Remove from the oven and leave to cool in the tin, then turn out. If you want to glaze the cake, make up the apricot glaze by diluting the apricot jam with a little water and then heating it gently in a saucepan, stirring until smooth. Pour the warm glaze through a sieve and brush it immediately over the top of the cake.

A tiny old lady, round as a barrel, ran the smallest, most magical shop in Minori. With a stern expression, she presided over a fabulous array of sweets, chocolates, and small pastries, but there was a kindly twinkle in her small, dark eyes.

Her shop was scarcely bigger than a telephone box, yet it was packed with an amazing variety of tantalizing delicacies. Everything was handmade. We children thought she was magic, and believed our parents when they told us that a fairy worked with her, sprinkling fairy dust over her sweets.

Pastries were filled with pâtisserie cream made from eggs that had been laid that morning, and flavored with chocolate. There were tarts filled with ricotta and cherries, apples and cream, and all kinds of fruit. There was nougat, too, made with sugar, almonds, and honey. The little *signora* stood with her arms folded across her chest, the trays of sweets before her covered in white muslin cloths. It was pure theater. She waited until we were breathless with anticipation before lifting the muslin very slowly to reveal the mouth-watering displays and release the most tantalizing smells.

I was lucky. I had the chance to taste her sweets now and then because my grandfather would send me on errands to her shop and always gave me a little extra money for myself. The fairy lady always chanted: "What do you want? How much have you got? Has your grandad sent you?" When I close my eyes, I can still hear her. She would wrap my grandfather's order in beautiful crisp, colored paper. And then she would make a smaller parcel for me. She seemed to read my mind, and always put in the very sweets I had been fantasizing about. Needless to say, my parcel was opened and devoured almost as soon as I left the shop.

biscotti rococo
spicy almond cookies

This is an old recipe from Naples. The exotic spices reflect the type of ingredients introduced to ancient Naples by the Arabic invasions. In fact, these cookies taste more like a North African specialty than an Italian one. Stored in an airtight container, they will keep for about two weeks. They are delicious served at teatime, or after dinner as an alternative to the classic Tuscan *cantuccini*, for dipping into a dessert wine such as Passito di Pantelleria or Vin Santo.

makes about 40

2½ cups/11 oz/300 g all-purpose flour
2 cups/7 oz/200 g ground almonds
1 cup/7 oz/200 g sugar
1 envelope/¼ oz/10 g instant yeast
2 tbsp/1 oz/25 g butter, diced
2 tbsp finely grated lemon zest
2 tbsp finely grated orange zest
⅔ cup/150 ml sweet white wine
1 egg, beaten, plus beaten egg,
    for brushing
5 oz/150 g mixed candied peel,
    finely chopped
1 cup/5⅓ oz/150 g whole almonds,
    roughly chopped
1 tsp ground cinnamon
a pinch of ground nutmeg
1 egg, beaten, for brushing
confectioner's sugar, for dusting

Preheat the oven to 350°F/180°C. Mix the flour, ground almonds, sugar, and yeast together in a large bowl. Add the butter and rub it in with your fingertips until the mixture resembles breadcrumbs. Add the lemon and orange zests, wine, egg, candied peel, almonds, cinnamon, and nutmeg and mix well, preferably with your hands, to form a soft dough. Form into golf-ball shapes, then, on a lightly floured surface, roll into sausage shapes 5–6 in/12.5–15 cm long. Shape each one into a ring, overlapping the ends slightly and pressing them together to seal (like mini bagels).

Place on baking trays lined with parchment paper and brush with the beaten egg. Bake for 20–25 minutes, until golden brown. Dust with confectioner's sugar and serve.

salsina picante con pere

pear and chili relish

This wonderfully tangy relish makes a perfect accompaniment to very mature hard cheese such as Pecorino, or a selection of after-dinner cheeses. It also goes well with cold meats. Apart from grilling the pears, there is no cooking involved. Stored in attractive jars, the relish makes an ideal present, together with a hunk of good-quality hard cheese.

makes about 1 quart/2¼ lb/1 kg
3 pears, weighing about 12 oz/350 g
confectioner's sugar for dusting
4 large, fresh medium-hot red chili
   peppers, roughly chopped
1 lb 2 oz/500 g mostarda di Cremona
   (preferably the hot variety, see
   page 203), any seeds removed
generous 1 cup/13 oz/375 g marmalade,
   preferably thick-cut

Cut the pears in half and core them. Cut in half again and then again. Cut into $1/_{12}$ in/2 mm cubes. Arrange on a large, flat baking tray and dust all over with confectioner's sugar. Place under a hot broiler for about 10 minutes, until the pears have caramelized.

Meanwhile, place the chilies, mostarda di Cremona, and marmalade in a food processor and whiz until smooth (if you are using fine-cut marmalade, don't add it to the food processor). Transfer to a large bowl (fine-cut marmalade should be mixed in now). Add the caramelized pears and mix well.

Fill one large or several small storage jars with the mixture. It will keep for a couple of months in the fridge.

Formaggi
an Italian cheese selection

Cheese can be served before or instead of dessert, and although more popular eaten this way in northern Italy it is now also becoming the trend in the South. Traditionally in the South, cheese is consumed as part of the antipasto course.

I love the cheese course, which is often the highlight of a meal. There are so many varieties and you can combine them with different accompaniments to make it a real talking point. When buying cheese, look out for fully ripened, good-quality specimens, even if you have to travel a little to buy the best. I always bring back some cheese from Italy, since several excellent local types are not available elsewhere. Nevertheless, you can get many good varieties in Italian delicatessens and specialist cheese shops nowadays.

Here are some tips on serving cheese as part of an Italian meal.

Take the cheese out of the fridge and leave it at room temperature for about 4 hours before serving. This softens it and its flavor becomes more pronounced.

If serving cheese as part of an antipasto, use a fresh one such as buffalo mozzarella, drizzled with lots of extra virgin olive oil, scamorza, or caprino (Italian goat cheese).

To make up a selection, choose a couple of hard cheeses, such as Parmesan and Pecorino, a semi-soft cheese such as Taleggio or provolone, and two soft cheeses—one blue-veined, such as gorgonzola or dolcelatte, and one plain, such as caprino. Four or five cheeses are sufficient; too many and the tastebuds get confused. Serve with some *taralli* (a southern Italian, crisp, twice-baked breadstick-like cracker), fresh bread, or plain crackers and some fresh fruit or celery. Always accompany with a good red wine or a full-bodied white.

If you serve just one cheese after dinner, it should be something quite special, such as Castelmagno or Formaggio di fossa served with my special chili relish (see opposite). Alternatively, a good-quality gorgonzola or dolcelatte drizzled with honey and served with a few walnuts is a great way to end a meal.

Good accompaniments to cheese include pears, grapes, walnuts, and fresh fava beans.

Mostarda di Cremona is also excellent with cheese. This is a preserve made of candied fruits and mustard and is available in mild and hot versions. It can be bought in jars from good Italian delicatessens.

Index

A

agnolotti filled with meat 34
almonds: semifreddo of almonds and
    white chocolate 190
    spicy almond cookies 198
Amalfi lemon tart 184
anchovies 12
    mozzarella and anchovy skewers 154
antipasto of fresh peaches and
    prosciutto 98
artichokes 139
    salad of raw artichokes, asparagus,
      and fennel 135
    stuffed globe artichokes 128
arugula: sea bass with arugula 82
    tagliatelle with tuna, lemon, and
      arugula 46
asparagus: potato gnocchi filled with
    asparagus 64
    salad of raw artichokes, asparagus, and
      fennel 135

B

beef: agnolotti filled with meat 34
    steamed meatballs 98
    stuffed beef rolls in tomato ragu 100
beets, marinated 136
borlotti bean soup, fresh 22
bread 169–79
    basic bread dough 172
    bread with salami, cheese, and eggs 174
    breadcrumbs 172
    bruschetta 116, 155
    crostini 155
    focaccia with garlic and rosemary 176
    mixed grilled vegetable and Parmesan
      rolls 177
broth, chicken 16
bruschetta 116, 155

C

cakes: chocolate and red wine cake 194
    pear cake 196
carpaccio of smoked mozzarella
    cheese 156
celery 139
cheese 12, 13
    baked eggplant rolls filled with
      mozzarella 134
    baked pasta shells filled with cheese 36
    basic polenta with cheese 55
    bread with salami, cheese, and eggs 174
    carpaccio of smoked mozzarella
      cheese 156
    deep-fried stuffed rice balls 162
    eggplant slices with a Parmesan and
      polenta crust 130
    genuine Neapolitan pizza 164
    Italian cheese selection 201
    leek and onion omelet rolls in a
      Parmesan crust 166
    mixed grilled vegetable and Parmesan
      rolls 177
    mozzarella and anchovy skewers 154
    spaghetti with fava beans, cherry
      tomatoes, and goat cheese 38
    see also ricotta cheese
chicken: baby chicken in a cider vinegar
    sauce 108
    chicken bites wrapped in pancetta and
      sage 111
    chicken breasts with lemon and
      thyme 110
    chicken broth 16
chickpea purée 122
chili peppers 12
    jumbo shrimp and crab with garlic
      and chili 90
    pear and chili relish 200
chocolate: chocolate and red wine
    cake 194
    chocolate cake topping 194
    semifreddo of almonds and white
      chocolate 190
compote: dried fruit compote with
    rum 186
cookies, spicy almond 198
crab: jumbo shrimp and crab with garlic
    and chili 90
    linguine with crab 40
crostini 155

D

dried fruit compote with rum 186
duck breasts in limoncello 112

E

eggs: bread with salami, cheese, and

eggs 174
   leek and onion omelet rolls in a
     Parmesan crust 166
   tomato soup with whisked egg
     whites 25
eggplants: baked eggplant rolls filled
   with mozzarella 134
   eggplant slices with a Parmesan and
     polenta crust 130

F

fava beans: risotto with fresh peas, fava
   beans, and zucchini 60
   spaghetti with fava beans, cherry
     tomatoes, and goat cheese 38
   stuffed fava bean cakes 158
fennel: orange and fennel salad 122
   rolled swordfish fillet with fennel 81
   salad of raw artichokes, asparagus, and
     fennel 135
fish 71–93
   preserved fish 93
   see also hake; trout, *etc*
focaccia with garlic and rosemary 176

G

game 95–6, 112–17
garlic 12, 139
   focaccia with garlic and rosemary 176
   jumbo shrimp and crab with garlic
     and chili 90
   rabbit with garlic and rosemary 116
gnocchi 53, 63–9
   pasta dumplings served with tomato
     and basil sauce 69
   polenta gnocchi with a red and
     yellow pepper sauce 56

potato gnocchi filled with asparagus 64
   pumpkin gnocchi baked with butter
     and sage 68
   sun-dried tomato gnocchi with black
     olive sauce 66
grapes, sweet tart with harvest 178
green beans: hake salad with green beans
   and salsa verde 74
   trofie with pesto, green beans, and
     potatoes 44
guinea fowl: breast of guinea fowl stuffed
   with herbs 114
   guinea fowl with pancetta and
     raisins 115

H

hake salad with green beans and salsa
   verde 74
halibut: halibut with caper and dill
     sauce 77
   halibut with lemon and butter 77
herbs 12
   breast of guinea fowl stuffed with
     herbs 114
   grilled lamb chops filled with
     prosciutto and herbs 102

I

ice cream, limoncello and strawberry 188
ingredients 12–13

K

kale: potato and Tuscan kale bake 125

L

lamb: grilled lamb chops filled with
   prosciutto and herbs 102
leek and onion omelet rolls in a
   Parmesan crust 166
lemons: Amalfi lemon tart 184
   chicken breasts with lemon and
     thyme 110
   halibut with lemon and butter 77
   ravioli filled with ricotta and lemon 37
   tagliatelle with tuna, lemon, and
     arugula 46
lentil soup 24
limoncello: duck breasts in limoncello 112
   limoncello and strawberry ice
     cream 188

M

meat 95–119
   preserved meats 118
   steamed meatballs 98
   see also beef; lamb, *etc*
mushrooms 12, 139, 147
   penne with mushrooms, shrimp, and
     saffron 43
   preserved mushrooms 149
   puffball cutlets 149
   sauté of mixed wild mushrooms 148
   tagliatelle with mixed mushrooms 150
mussels: stuffed mussels with tomato
   sauce 86

N

Neapolitan Easter wheat and ricotta tart
   193
Neapolitan pizza 164

O

octopus, stewed 84

oils 12–13

olives 13

   sun-dried tomato gnocchi with black olive sauce 66

omelet rolls, leek and onion 166

onions 139

   leek and onion omelet rolls 166

   veal slow-cooked with onions 99

orange and fennel salad 122

P

pancetta: chicken bites wrapped in pancetta and sage 111

   farfalle with peas, pancetta, and ricotta 51

   guinea fowl with pancetta and raisins 115

panna cotta, fresh mint 192

parsley 139

pasta 12, 27–51

   agnolotti filled with meat 34

   baked pasta shells filled with cheese 36

   basic pasta dough 30

   eggless fresh pasta 30

   farfalle with peas, pancetta, and ricotta 51

   linguine with crab 40

   pasta dumplings served with tomato and basil sauce 69

   pasta snacks 160

   penne with mushrooms, shrimp, and saffron 43

   pennette with zucchini flowers 50

   ravioli filled with ricotta and lemon 37

spaghetti with fava beans, cherry tomatoes, and goat cheese 38

tagliatelle with mixed mushrooms 150

tagliatelle with tuna, lemon, and arugula 46

tagliolini with black truffle 47

trofie with pesto, green beans, and potatoes 44

peaches: antipasto of fresh peaches and prosciutto 98

pears: pear and chili relish 200

   pear cake 196

peas: deep-fried stuffed rice balls 162

   farfalle with peas, pancetta, and ricotta 51

   pea and fresh mint soup 18

   risotto with fresh peas, fava beans, and zucchini 60

peppers 139

   polenta gnocchi with a red and yellow pepper sauce 56

   stuffed baby peppers 126

   sweet and sour peppers 126

pesto: trofie with pesto, green beans, and potatoes 44

pizza, Neapolitan 164

polenta 53–7

   basic polenta with cheese 55

   eggplant slices with a Parmesan and polenta crust 130

   grilled polenta 55

   polenta gnocchi with a red and yellow pepper sauce 56

pork: agnolotti filled with meat 34

   stuffed rolled pork belly 106

potatoes 139

   potato and Tuscan kale bake 125

potato gnocchi filled with asparagus 64

sautéed potatoes 124

sun-dried tomato gnocchi 66

trofie with pesto, green beans, and potatoes 44

warm potato salad 124

poultry 95–6, 108–11

prosciutto di Parma: antipasto of fresh peaches and prosciutto 98

   grilled lamb chops filled with prosciutto and herbs 102

pumpkin gnocchi baked with butter and sage 68

R

rabbit with garlic and rosemary 116

ragu, stuffed beef rolls in tomato 100

raisins, guinea fowl with pancetta and 115

ravioli filled with ricotta and lemon 37

red wine: chocolate and red wine cake 194

relish, pear and chili 200

rice: basic risotto 58

   deep-fried stuffed rice balls 162

   risotto with fresh peas, fava beans, and zucchini 60

   risotto with sorrel 61

   southern Italian risotto with vegetables 62

ricotta cheese: farfalle with peas, pancetta, and ricotta 51

   Neapolitan Easter wheat and ricotta tart 193

   ravioli filled with ricotta and lemon 37

   stuffed fava bean cakes 158

risotto 53, 58–62

   basic risotto 58

risotto with fresh peas, fava beans, and zucchini 60

risotto with sorrel 61

southern Italian risotto with vegetables 62

rolls, mixed grilled vegetable and Parmesan 177

rum, dried fruit compote with 186

S

salads 139

hake salad with green beans and salsa verde 74

orange and fennel salad 122

salad of raw artichokes, asparagus, and fennel 135

warm potato salad 124

zucchini salad with fresh mint 135

salami 118

bread with salami, cheese, and eggs 174

salsa verde 74

salt 13

sauces: "fresh" canned tomato sauce 143

fresh tomato sauce 142

heavy-based tomato sauce 143

light basic tomato sauce 142

sea bass with arugula 82

sea bream: sea bream fillets in a honey and white wine vinegar sauce 80

whole sea bream cooked with cherry tomatoes 78

semifreddo of almonds and white chocolate 190

shrimp: jumbo shrimp and crab with garlic and chili 90

penne with mushrooms, shrimp, and saffron 43

shellfish 71–93

skewers, mozzarella and anchovy 154

sorrel, risotto with 61

soups 15–25

chicken broth 16

fresh borlotti bean soup 22

lentil soup 24

mixed root vegetable soup 20

pea and fresh mint soup 18

tomato soup with whisked egg whites 25

stock 13

strawberries: fresh strawberries with strawberry sauce 187

limoncello and strawberry ice cream 188

swordfish: rolled swordfish fillet with fennel 81

T

tarts: Amalfi lemon tart 184

Neapolitan Easter wheat and ricotta tart 193

sweet tart with harvest grapes 178

tomatoes 139, 141

"fresh" canned tomato sauce 143

fresh tomato sauce 142

genuine Neapolitan pizza 164

heavy-based tomato sauce 143

light basic tomato sauce 142

pasta dumplings served with tomato and basil sauce 69

spaghetti with fava beans, cherry tomatoes, and goat cheese 38

stuffed beef rolls in tomato ragu 100

stuffed mussels with tomato sauce 86

sun-dried tomato gnocchi with black olive sauce 66

tomato soup with whisked egg whites 25

whole sea bream cooked with cherry tomatoes 78

trout, raw marinated 76

truffle, tagliolini with black 47

tuna: tagliatelle with tuna, lemon, and arugula 46

V

veal, slow-cooked with onions 99

vegetables 12, 121–51

Gennaro's vegetable cooking tips 139

grilled vegetables 132

mixed grilled vegetable and Parmesan rolls 177

mixed preserved vegetables 138

mixed root vegetable soup 20

southern Italian risotto with vegetables 62

vinegar 13

W

wine: chocolate and red wine cake 194

Z

zucchini 139

zucchini salad with fresh mint 135

risotto with fresh peas, fava beans, and zucchini 60

stuffed zucchini parcels 129

zucchini flowers, pennette with 50

First published in 2017 by
INTERLINK BOOKS
An imprint of Interlink Publishing Group, Inc.
46 Crosby Street, Northampton, MA 01060
www.interlinkbooks.com

Text © Gennaro Contaldo, 2017
Design and layout © Pavilion Books
Company Ltd, 2017
Photography © Pavilion Books Company
Ltd, 2017, except where credited otherwise
American edition copyright © Interlink
Publishing Group, Inc, 2017

All recipe photography by Kim Lightbody
Photograph on p. 2 © Patrice Hauser/Getty
Images, pp.10–11 © Atlantide Phototravel/
Getty Images, p.89 © Glenn Beanland/Getty
Images, p.183 © Larry Gatz/Getty Images;
on p.28 © The Stapleton Collection;
on pp. 4–5, 21, 42, 52, 73, 97, 105, 119, 152,
160, 167, 168, 173 © Gennaro Contaldo

Library of Congress Cataloging-in-
Publication Data available
ISBN 978-1-56656-027-6

10 9 8 7 6 5 4 3 2 1

Reproduction by Mission, Hong Kong
Printed and bound by 1010 Printing
International Ltd, China

To request our 48-page, full-color catalog,
please call us toll free at 1-800-238-LINK,
visit www.interlinkbooks.com, or send us an
e-mail at: info@interlinkbooks.com.

acknowledgments

Thank you to Sarah Walmsley for patiently listening to all my stories and putting
them to paper so beautifully; to Liz Przybylski for spending many hours in the
kitchen with me, taking down the recipes and writing them up; to Heather Holden-
Brown for her enthusiasm throughout the project and for being such fun
in Italy!; to Jane Middleton, for being so thorough in checking and rechecking all
the text; and to Jo Roberts-Miller for all her hard work and efficiency in putting
the book together. To Steve and Janice Lanning for the great idea. Thank you also
to Luigi Bonomi, my agent, for making this happen!

Thank you to Adriana Contaldo, for helping to cook the recipes on the shoots; to
Emily Ezekiel for superb food and prop styling; to Kim Lightbody, the photographer,
for the most beatiful photographs; and finally to all the Pavilion team, especially our
editor Emily Preece-Morrison, and designers Laura Russell and Rosamund Saunders.